MANAGING PERFORMANCE

Managing Performance

Goals, Feedback, Coaching, Recognition

JENNY HILL

Gower Management Workbooks

Published by
Gower Publishing Limited
Gower House
Croft Road
Aldershot
Hampshire GU11 3HR
England

Gower
Old Post Road
Brookfield
Vermont 05036
USA

British Library Cataloguing in Publication Data

Hill, Jenny
Managing performance: goals, feedback, coaching, recognition, – (Gower management workbooks)
1. Supervision of employees 2. Performance standards 3. Goal setting in personnel management
I. Title
658.3'124

ISBN 0 566 07739 6

Typeset by Wileman Design and printed in Great Britain by Hartnolls Ltd, Bodmin.

Contents

This Part will show you how to set robust goals for yourself and your team.

Part I supports the following Units and Elements of the 1997 MCI Management Standards Level 4.

- *Develop your own resources, Unit C.2, Element C.2.2.*
- *Manage the performance of teams and individuals, Unit C.13, Element C.13.1, 13.2.*

PART II GIVING AND RECEIVING FEEDBACK

This Part will show you how to give regular feedback to individuals and teams and manage a formal review.

Part II supports the following Units and Elements of 1997 MCI Management Standards Level 4.

- *Develop teams and individuals to enhance performance, Unit C.10, C.10.5.*
- *Manage the performance of teams and individuals, Unit C.13, Elements C.13.3, C.13.4.*
- *Respond to poor performance in your team, Unit C.15, Element C.15.1.*

PART III MANAGING COACHING ASSIGNMENTS

This Part will show you how to manage coaching assignments and meetings skilfully.

Part III supports the following Units and Elements of 1997 MCI Management Standards Level 4.

- *Develop teams and individuals to enhance performance, Unit C.10, Elements C.10.4*
- *Manage the performance of teams and individuals, Unit C.13, Element C.13.1*

PART IV RECOGNIZING SUCCESS

This Part will show you how to recognize individual and team successes and thank people memorably.

Part IV supports the following Units and Elements of 1997 MCI Standards Level 4.

- *Develop teams and individuals to enhance performance, Unit C.10, Element C.10.3.*
- *Manage the performance of teams and individuals, Unit C.13, Element C.13.4.*

Skillscan

You can identify your current skill level and select your priority learning areas with Skillscan. Complete the activity by circling your current skill level for each of the topics listed below.

Identify your current skill level and select your priority learning areas from the contents list below:	**Circle your current skill level:**				
	Low				***High***
PART I SETTING GOALS					
• Assessing the need for clear goals	1	2	3	4	5
• Describing clear goals and their measures for success	1	2	3	4	5
• Involving others in helping you achieve goals	1	2	3	4	5
• Planning the time and costs involved in achieving your goals	1	2	3	4	5
• Evaluating the outcomes	1	2	3	4	5
PART II GIVING AND RECEIVING FEEDBACK					
• Getting feedback from teams	1	2	3	4	5
• Giving feedback to teams	1	2	3	4	5
• Getting feedback from colleagues	1	2	3	4	5
• Managing and conducting formal performance review	1	2	3	4	5
PART III MANAGING COACHING ASSIGNMENTS					
• Choosing coaching assignments	1	2	3	4	5
• Managing coaching assignments	1	2	3	4	5
• Conducting coaching sessions	1	2	3	4	5
PART IV RECOGNIZING SUCCESS					
• Recognizing and thanking individuals for good performance	1	2	3	4	5
• Recognizing and thanking teams for good performance	1	2	3	4	5

Introduction

Successful organizations attract managers who see opportunities to develop the skills, knowledge and experience of all their staff. They will risk letting junior members learn more and develop the expertise and the skill to deal directly with customers and suppliers whilst taking responsibility for whole tasks. These organizations are today's learning organizations. They are intent on growing fast and seizing market opportunities. They are peopled with individuals also intent on growing fast and seizing learning opportunities.

Many organizations are still staffed with Russian Dolls – senior managers who do not share status, skill, knowledge and experience with middle managers who in turn do not share their status, skill, knowledge and experience with their supervisors. The outcome is corporate thrombosis which commonly presents itself as a lack of communication.

Learning organizations do not reflect this hierarchy of compressed opportunities. Today's organizations are increasingly managing information, and exploiting people's intelligence. In a service society we no longer employ hired hands and manage people's labour; we now hire minds and develop people's potential. Successful managers are those who generously communicate their skills, knowledge and experience. This Workbook will not only help you do just this, it will also help you manage people so they can develop within their jobs.

Part I Setting Goals shows you how to set effective goals with individuals and teams.

Part II Giving and Receiving Feedback gives you quick access to skills for getting and giving informal feedback and for managing performance review.

Part III Managing Coaching Assignments provides you with a clear framework for coaching others and gaining their involvement.

Part IV Recognizing Success offers you insights and ideas for recognizing and thanking people for their contribution.

Together the four Parts will provide you with skills for managing performance. Used independently, each Part is sufficiently flexible to support or develop your current management style.

How to Get the Most from this Workbook

This Workbook has been designed to be used by busy managers at work. It will help you to improve your own managing skills while you manage and develop individuals within your team if you need to:

- set goals for others
- give and receive feedback informally or as part of a formal performance review process
- delegate tasks and coach individuals to undertake them
- recognize success in a rewarding or motivating manner.

Each Part has been designed in the same way so that you can:

- use the **Fast Track** pages to gain ideas and insights about managing intelligence and improving performance
- use the **Skillbuilder** pages to build you skills in specific areas.

To obtain a quick overview of the topic covered in each Part, you need only go through the Fast Track pages. In this way, you should be able to complete each Part in less than one hour.

To use the Workbook as a systematic, self-development package, complete the Skillbuilder activities. You can use the **Skillscan** on page ix to identify specific topics and programme your learning.

Skillbuilder activities comprise questionnaires and activities which you can complete on the page or at work with your colleagues. You can plan future action by completing the **Action Points** at the end of each chapter, whilst the **Check Points** provide a summary of each chapter.

The frameworks for goal-setting, formal feedback and coaching provide you with a complete agenda for undertaking these activities. Model questions for conducting a performance review and a coaching assignment will give support to first-timers and a useful check for experienced managers.

The whole Workbook gives you a complete self-development programme for managing performance: selecting parts of it will help you acquire or update skills.

PART I
Setting Goals

Setting realistic goals is a skill which will enable you to actively manage the performance of people at work and develop their jobs for them.

In setting goals we define the future and allow others to *achieve success*. This first Part includes **ACHIEVE**, a framework for goal-setting, taking you through six steps which will enable you to define, measure and monitor realistic performance goals for yourself and others.

Part I helps you identify robust goals for your team and yourself by giving you:

- quick access to the skills involved in setting realistic goals
- a six-step framework for building clear performance goals
- insights and practical ideas for obtaining a clear focus on the future.

UNIT 1 Focusing on the Future

In this unit you will:

- **consider people's different kinds of focus on the future**
- **consider how they balance their differences**
- **assess the different kinds of focus on the future which you and your team members hold.**

We experience success by looking backwards but we create it by looking forward and having a clear focus on the future. People focus on the future in different ways and it is this focus that determines how we set our goals.

❖ **Some of us are dreamers.**
Inspired by emotion, dreamers have a hazy focus on the future and do not define their goals sharply.

❖ **Some of us are ambitious.**
Ambitious people tend to plan years ahead and, like dreamers, are inspired by emotion to carry themselves forward. Ambitious people always visualize and describe their goals clearly.

❖ **Some of us are goal-setters.**
People who are goal-driven plan for action. They plan months ahead and define clear goals and outcomes for themselves.

❖ **Some of us are task-drivers.**
Task-drivers are also driven by action, but by today's action. Their goals are immediate and urgent. These people feel that tomorrow is another day.

Our dreams principally engage our emotions and tend to be long-term (*I dream of living in France when I retire*) whereas our targets tend to be short-term and based on specific actions (*Are we on target to get that order out today?*). It is important to keep a balance – our targets provide us with roots to grow and our dreams with wings to fly. Too much emphasis on targets can result in action without direction. Too much dreaming can mean that you will drift forever.

In this unit you will:

- consider people's different kinds of focus on the future
- consider how they balance their differences
- assess the different kinds of focus on the future which you and your team members hold

Balancing Differences

Do you have your nose to the grindstone or eyes on the hills? Ask others how far ahead they look when they set goals. Tomorrow, next week, next month, or next year?

Your team are individuals whose focus on the future will naturally differ. This can cause difficulties in setting and achieving goals.

The matrix below highlights some of the problems that may arise in team goal-setting where team members have different views of the future and, therefore, different motivations.

	DREAMER	AMBITIOUS	GOAL-SETTER	TASK-DRIVEN
A DREAMER with a . . .	There's a danger of all talk and no action			
An AMBITIOUS person with a . . .	There's a danger of the vision being subservient to ambition	There's a danger of destructive competitiveness		
A GOAL-SETTER with a . . .	There's a danger of frustration if goals are lacking clear definition	There's a danger of frustration if ambition is tied down by rational goals or, conversely, if goals are diverted to achieve the ambitions of the other person	There's a danger of lack of motivation if the approach becomes too coldly rational	
A TASK-DRIVEN person with a . . .	There's a danger of completely different views of time and the future	There's a danger of frustration as those who are task-driven hold back ambitious people	There's a danger of goals lacking sufficient scope if limited by short-term tasks	There's a danger of being highly blinkered and unaware of approaching threats and opportunities

YOU MAY NOW CONTINUE WITH THE NEXT FAST TRACK SECTION ON PAGE 13
OR MOVE TO THE SKILLBUILDER EXERCISE ON PAGE 7

Focusing on the Future

Before setting goals you will find it useful to assess the future focus that both you and your team adopt when setting goals. Ask each person on your team (including yourself) to complete the following questionnaire.

Get each person including yourself to score themselves according to Answer Box 1 at the end of Unit 1. Consider the implications for yourself and discuss with your team the similarities/differences and their implications.

Questionnaire Circle one answer to each of the following questions.

1. When asked where you want to be in five years' time do you
- **a.** say it's too far away for you to have any clear view?
- **b.** describe the sorts of things you wish you could be doing?
- **c.** describe your objectives?
- **d.** talk passionately about the things you want to achieve and how you are going to do them?

2. If you were convinced that the world was going to end in one year's time, would you
- **a.** sit down and reappraise what you want to complete in the year?
- **b.** plan each day carefully to get the most out of it?
- **c.** regret not having done the things you'd like to do?
- **d.** give up whatever you are doing to do those things you always wanted to?

3. The day after the world was supposed to end but didn't, would you
- **a.** carry on with your new lifestyle?
- **b.** sit down and adjust your plans to the new situation?
- **c.** think about where you wanted to be?
- **d.** laugh with relief and set about getting back to where you wanted to be?

4. Are you the sort of person who
- **a.** has mapped out your future and how you are going to achieve it?
- **b.** always knows exactly what you will be doing next week?
- **c.** is prepared just to take life as it comes?
- **d.** has a good idea of what you will be doing next week but a better one of what you should be achieving next month?

5. Do you mostly believe in
- **a.** letting things happen?
- **b.** making things happen?
- **c.** planning what should happen?
- **d.** making sure it has happened?

For a diagnosis of your responses see Answer Box 1.1 on page 9.

SKILLBUILDER

Focusing on the Future

Here are some guidelines for sharing the same time horizons.

- Ask your team members to sort the goals which they are trying to achieve into categories – long-term/medium-term/short-term/now
- Discuss the results and develop a shared view of what should be in each category.

Because goals provide a bridge to the future it is important to describe our dreams and clarify our ambitions in order to set real goals and achieve important tasks. We must also define what is a dream, an ambition, a goal and a task.

ACTION POINTS

At work I
- dream that . . .
- have ambitions to . . .
- set goals for . . .
- achieve tasks that achieve . . .

ANSWER BOX 1.1

Use the following matrix to score yourself according to the opinion you selected for each question in the questionnaire 'Focusing on the Future'.

Question	*Answer*				*Score*
	a	**b**	**c**	**d**	
1	4	1	3	2	
2	3	4	2	1	
3	1	3	4	2	
4	2	4	1	3	
5	1	2	3	4	
				Total	

Enter your score on the grid below to see which category you fall into:

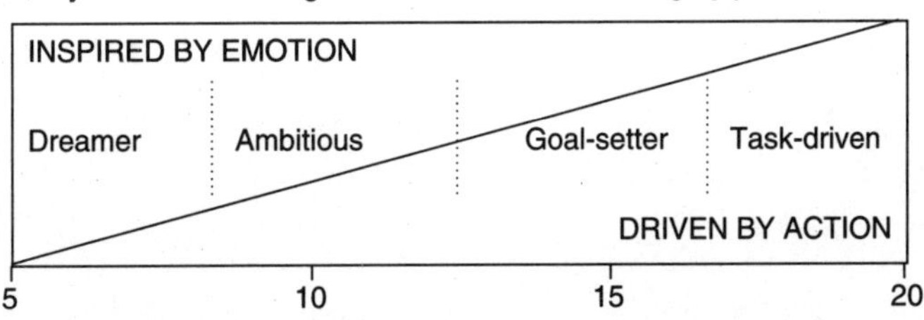

CHECK POINTS

UNIT 2 ACHIEVE Realistic Goals

In this unit you will learn a systematic approach to setting realistic goals at work. It is based on a six-step framework summarized on to one page which you will be able to use as

- **a project plan for yourself and/or your team**
- **a brief for a coaching assignment**
- **a summary for allocating time and money in priority areas.**

The six-step framework for defining a goal

In order to achieve success we have to set realistic goals. Realistic goals are robust and carry us to the future. They can be defined using the six-step framework which will make sure that you cover all the important angles and include all the important people on your journey to success. The six steps that make up **ACHIEVE** are:

Assess the present
CHart the future
Identify measures for success
Embrace others
Verify the timetable
Evaluate

Step 1: Assess the Present

Achieving any goal implies **change** – a change from the current situation to some future one. To define that change you and your team must know the current situation. The more accurately you can assess what needs to change, the better your chances of success. Identifying current strengths, weaknesses, opportunities and threats is a useful exercise.

EXAMPLE

Kim Bailey is Customer Services Manager for a facilities management company. She leads a team of four customer service personnel. She and her team have identified a number of key **weaknesses and threats** – low customer satisfaction with the portering and catering services the company offers.

They put a poster on their office noticeboard divided into

Strengths	Weaknesses
Opportunities	Threats

Over a week they each thought about and selected issues to place under each heading. A key **weakness** was that customer complaints about the quality of service had risen by 25 per cent over the last year and were now running at over 10 per month. A significant **threat** was that one important customer had switched to a competitor. The business was in danger of losing further customers unless the quality of service improved significantly.

Define your goal. Success doesn't come to you – you go to it.

Kim Bailey and her team also identified some **strengths**, such as an experienced team able to identify the key weaknesses. A new catering services supervisor, who seemed keen to listen to customer opinions and improve, also appeared to be a **strength**. There was also an **opportunity** for her to coach the task-oriented portering services manager.

YOU MAY NOW CONTINUE WITH THE NEXT FAST TRACK SECTION ON PAGE 14
OR MOVE TO THE SKILLBUILDER EXERCISE ON PAGE 19

Step 2: Chart the Future

A clear vision of your destination is as critical as knowing where you are to start from. Unless you can 'see' your desired end result you will have difficulty in achieving it. You need to visualize with your team the common future you and they want to achieve.

VISUALIZE SUCCESS
As part of their training athletes learn how to 'see' themselves making their winning leap or crossing the finishing line first.

EXAMPLE

Kim Bailey and her team created a vision of the future that included:

- the complaints file lying empty
- contract teams communicating concerns urgently
- letters of customer commendation posted on the wall
- an important new contract signed, sealed and delivered.

Once you have described the current position and pictured the future, you can begin to decide exactly what needs to change.

EXAMPLE

To achieve their vision Kim Bailey and her team identified three areas where they needed to achieve results.

We need to change . . .	in order to . . .	by . . .
• the low levels of product knowledge and operational skills of our contract teams	• develop qualified and recognized experts in their professional and technical areas so that we can exhibit the skills and knowledge necessary in competing for new business and winning customer approval	• putting in place a team training programme that will raise levels of product knowledge, technical skill and customer awareness. It will provide operational customer service simulations to help teams develop their operational skills
• the frequent delays in responding to customer concerns	• be able to identify and respond to all our customer concerns within two days. Addressing concerns before they become complaints will save time and improve customer relations	• re-engineering the process by which customer concerns are communicated to management
• our inability to meet our commitment to the rapid repair of the equipment for which we are responsible	• be able to achieve a 24-hour response 100 per cent of the time and improve our communication	• setting in place a repair and replacement system that is speedy and reliable

YOU MAY NOW CONTINUE WITH THE NEXT FAST TRACK SECTION ON PAGE 15
OR MOVE TO THE SKILLBUILDER EXERCISE ON PAGE 20

FIX ON FEEDBACK
How does an orchestra measure the quality of its performance? Feedback from others can often provide the most objective measure of success. Where possible use an independent measure such as feedback from your customers – both internal or external.

Step 3: Identify Measures for Success

To know that you've achieved your goal you must not only be able to describe where you are and where you want to go (Step 2) but also establish ways of measuring your progress and ultimate success. This is often one of the most difficult parts of goal-setting. Ignore it and you'll never know if you succeeded and, more importantly, why.

EXAMPLE

Kim Bailey and her team established the following ways to measure their success.

The changes to be achieved were . . .	Success and progress were measured by . . .
• To develop contract teams as highly qualified and recognized experts in their profession and technical areas	• Starting all contract teams on a training programme leading to NVQ Level 3 in their specialist area
• To achieve a 100 per cent response to all customer concerns and complaints within two working days	• The development of a daily upward team briefing system. The measure of success is the number of new concerns being identified and percentage of very satisfied customers identified in the regular customer audit
• To achieve a 24-hour response for the rapid repair of equipment	• Redesigning equipment servicing logs with regular checks on all pieces of equipment and redesigning the equipment replacement schedule around usage not age.

YOU MAY NOW CONTINUE WITH THE NEXT FAST TRACK SECTION ON PAGE 16
OR MOVE TO THE SKILLBUILDER EXERCISE ON PAGE 21

Step 4: Embrace Others

Your goal will not be achieved in isolation. Your success will depend on support and input from others. You need to identify these people and the role they will play, or influence they will have, on your success.

EXAMPLE

Kim Bailey and her team identified the following groups and individuals as being critical to their success.

People involved	Role	Influence
• Director of Sales and Service	Controls budget	Power to veto or support any change proposals
• Three administrators	Liaise between customers and contract teams, passing on customer messages, etc.	Currently control flow of information between customers and contract teams
• Parts Dept. Manager	Responsible for repair policy	Power to veto or approve any repairs
• Contract Supervisors	Responsible for rostering teams, routine maintenance and job training	Authority, commitment and training skills – variable but crucial
• Human Resources Department	Gives advice and access to training skills and training budget	Instrumental in setting up training for service engineers

Spread the net wider than you first consider necessary – it is frustrating and costly to fail through lack of consultation. Shell Oil company spent much time and money in planning to dump the Brent Spar oil platform in deep water. The company gained the support of government and industry experts, but it was Greenpeace and German consumers who forced them to abandon their plans at the last moment.

YOU MAY NOW CONTINUE WITH THE NEXT FAST TRACK SECTION ON PAGE 17 OR MOVE TO THE SKILLBUILDER EXERCISE ON PAGE 22

Step 5: Verify the Time and Budget

GOING FOR GOAL
For athletes, the ultimate goal is a gold medal at the Olympics but this can be four years away. In order to work towards their goal they use a series of other events as staging posts in their build up.

A goal without a deadline and budget is not a goal, it's a dream.

If you don't give your goal a deadline you'll delay starting because something more urgent will always come up. If you don't budget you won't be able to resource your goal. You will give yourself added impetus to achieve your goal in time if you have a specific date and budget to work to. Deadlines set too far into the future will tempt you to put work off to a later date. If you set your deadline for more than six months ahead, consider establishing interim targets at shorter intervals. Reward yourself and the team for achieving them.

EXAMPLE

Kim Bailey and her team created the timescale and budget for achieving one of their goals – to implement a customer services training programme and set a start date for the programme.

A time and cost planner (see below) will give you signposts on your journey to success.

TIME AND COST PLANNER

Activity	Notes	Time		Expenditure	
		Budget	Actual	Budget	Actual
Budget approval	Sales and Service Director Human Resources Director	19 days		£10 700	
Briefing	Training Manager only	1 day		£300	
Analyse training needs	HR Department	2 days		£600	
Design programme	HR Department and Consultant	5 days		£1 500	
Programme appraisal	Training Manager	1 day		£300	
Implementation	HR Department and Consultant	10 days		£8 000	

YOU MAY NOW CONTINUE WITH THE NEXT FAST TRACK SECTION ON PAGE 18
OR MOVE TO THE SKILLBUILDER EXERCISE ON PAGE 23

FAST TRACK

Step 6: Evaluate

Life is best understood by examining yesterday. Opportunities happen tomorrow.

Having managed to define and plan your goal it is tempting to dash off and start working to achieve it. However, it is first wise to step back and run six brief checks to verify the suitability of your goal. Check that:

1. your goal is compatible with your organization's values
2. your goal is compatible with your operating environment
3. you have the ability to achieve it – in other words it is realistic
4. you can manage any positive or negative impact on other areas of the organization
5. your goal is compatible with other goals you, your team or department may have set
6. your goal is clear – that is, it will be understood by all involved.

YOU MAY NOW CONTINUE WITH THE NEXT FAST TRACK SECTION ON PAGE 31
OR MOVE TO THE SKILLBUILDER EXERCISE ON PAGE 24

Step 1: Assess the Present

Either on your own or with your team, develop an accurate and objective description of the current situation that you want to change. Some people think in words, others in pictures, so use whichever method works best for you in creating an accurate account. **Either** write down your description of the present situation.

The present situation is:

____

____

The strengths are:

____

____

The weaknesses are:

____

____

Potential threats from competition, technology or system changes are:

____

____

Opportunities could be:

____

____

Or, alternatively, draw a picture or diagram to describe it. Pictures are a good way to express the feelings in a situation.

Ask everyone to share their description so that you can develop an assessment that is agreed by everyone.

Step 2: Chart the Future

Get together with your team to develop an objective vision of where you want to be. It is important for everyone to agree about the future to prevent your team pulling in different directions.

Either ask each member to write down their vision.

____

____

____

____

____

____

Or ask them to draw a picture or diagram that describes it.

Ask everyone to share their vision so that you can develop a common view of where you want to be.

Then make an inventory of 'what' needs to change so you can describe 'how' to achieve your vision.

We need to change ...	in order to ...	by ...

This will form your action plan.

SKILLBUILDER

Step 3: Identify Measures for Success

Find a measure for each success you want to achieve.

People perform to targets but they should be the right ones. For example, if a customer satisfaction target is to reduce the number of complaints, it is simplicity itself to increase the measured level of customer satisfaction by throwing away all customer letters of complaint!

The changes to be achieved are . . .	Success and progress will be measured by . . .

Step 4: Embrace Others

List below the groups and individuals you regard as being critical to your success.

People involved	Role	Influence

You can now go one stage further.

- Assess the positive and negative impact of those you have identified.
- Plan how to make use of the positives and minimize the effect of the negatives.

Positives and negatives

People with positive influence are . . .	and can help by . . .
People with negative influence are . . .	and their influence can be minimized by . . .

Step 5: Verify the Time and Budget

Specify **by when** you need to achieve your goal, **the budget** for achieving the goal and, if appropriate, **the reward** for success. If you find it difficult to set a challenging timeframe or tend to put off getting started, decide on a significant reward. This must be something that you and your team really want.

Date for achievement and why:

Time budget:

Financial budget:

Reward:

Use this Time and Cost Planner to verify your time and budget.

TIME AND COST PLANNER

Activity	Notes	Time		Expenditure	
		Budget	Actual	Budget	Actual

SKILLBUILDER

Step 6: Evaluate

SKILLBUILDER

SIX QUICK CHECKS

1. This goal enhances my organization's values because it . . .

2. This goal is in harmony with my operating environment because . . .

3. This goal is realistic because it can be achieved by . . .

4. The positive impact of this goal can be enhanced by . . .
   The negative impacts can be minimized by . . .

5. This goal is . . .
   - compatible with . . .
   - in conflict with . . .

   This conflict can be resolved by . . .

6. This goal is well understood by people involved . . .
   I have checked it with . . .

ACHIEVE Realistic Goals

- Setting realistic goals will enable you to focus on the priorities that will enable you and your team to achieve success.
- Setting realistic goals defines useful projects which need to be managed. Think about combining them with coaching assignments.
- The skills for involving yourself with others through coaching are developed in Part III.

ACTION POINTS

Use this blank six-step framework to set your own goals. Keep it pinned up or in your desk diary. It will act as a project log and help to keep your eyes on the hills and your nose to the grindstone.

1. **A**ssess the present

2. **CH**art the future
   - the vision is to . . .
   - we need to change . . .
   - by . . .

3. **I**dentify measures for:
   - success . . .

CHECK POINTS

- changes . . .

- measured by . . .

4. **E**mbrace others:
   - people

   - role

   - influences

5. **V**erify the timescale and budget:
   - deadline

   - datelines

   - budget

6. **E**valuate

CHECK POINTS

PART II Giving and Receiving Feedback

Giving and receiving performance feedback, both informally on the job and formally as part of a performance review process, is critical to ensuring that the goals of the organization, the department, the individual are achieved and recognized.

Part II will enable you to manage the performance of people at work by giving you:

- quick access to the skills involved in giving regular and formal performance feedback
- a seven-step framework for managing formal performance feedback as part of performance review
- insights and practical ideas for giving and receiving feedback from people at work.

UNIT 3 Why Feedback is Important

In this unit we consider:

- **how effective feedback can enhance team performance and why it is so important for individual performance**
- **how performance review schemes have evolved and changed to meet current needs for employee involvement**
- **your own feedback style**

We influence people's performance by the way we give and receive feedback. There are three reasons why feedback is important:

For building confidence | *For building competence* | *For gaining contribution*

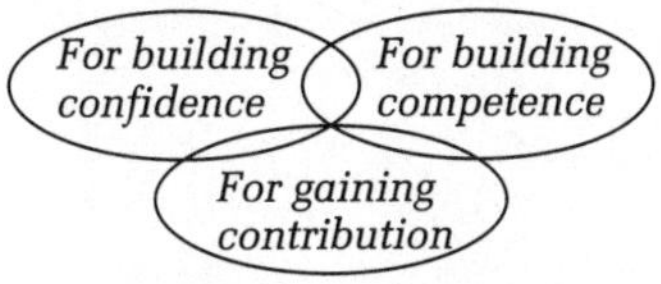

Feedback to build **confidence** usually comes in the form of praise.

'I was really pleased with the way you handled the project team today.'

It recognizes good performance and encourages more of the same behaviour. It is best delivered immediately after the event or task and builds confidence and self-esteem.

Feedback to develop **competence** lets a person know what needs to be done, why it should be done and how it should be done. If it is given immediately before the next performance of a task or activity it encourages better performance. If it's not to be perceived as a criticism, it must be given in the form of advice and at the right time.

'The next time you meet with this customer try asking more open questions. It will help you to identify his needs and match our product benefits more effectively.'

It is the balance of both kinds of feedback that helps people to manage their own performance and make an active **contribution** to the department's goals and success.

Effective Feedback

Feedback gives the opportunity to pay focused and fair attention to people at work.

- If done well it is a gift that is highly valued by the people you manage.
- If done badly it can disappoint, discourage and demotivate people.

Feedback is a gift that all managers must give and receive if they are to manage the performance of people at work effectively.

If it's to be a genuine gift, it must be given and packaged in a way that:

- helps people to improve, achieve and develop
- enhances people's strengths and contributions
- encourages people to manage their own performance
- builds self-esteem, confidence and job ownership.

Feedback helps people to build on their competence and manage their weaknesses.

To receive feedback from people which is helpful and constructive it should be:

- actively encouraged and sought
- received positively
- acted upon appropriately.

FEEDBACK LADDER

We all need feedback from others at work.
Write in the names of people who, at work, provide you with the different kinds of feedback listed below:

- Someone I can always rely on __________
- Someone who is always honest and open with me __________
- Someone I learn from __________
- Someone who makes me feel competent and valued __________
- Someone who gives me helpful ideas __________
- Someone who is always a source of valuable information __________
- Someone who will challenge me to take a good look at myself __________
- Someone I can share bad news with __________
- Someone I can share good news and good feelings with __________

YOU MAY NOW CONTINUE WITH THE NEXT FAST TRACK SECTION ON PAGE 32
OR MOVE TO THE SKILLBUILDER EXERCISE ON PAGE 35

Feedback Style

Feedback styles have moved from **controlling** the performance of others to **empowering** the performance of others. We now try not only to build confidence and competence, but also encourage contribution.

- A **controlling style** when assessing and appraising were popular feedback styles in the past.
- A great deal of talking and **closed questioning** by the assessor or appraiser was also a feature.
- An **open style** is now more popular; this style seeks feedback and features open questioning and active listening.

In the 1960s feedback was given to people via *staff assessments*. These assessments were rather like school reports or 'the boss knows best'. It was a formal, controlled process with an emphasis on **assessing** past performance, and usually linked to the salary review. The staff member was often not included.

During the 1970s feedback was generally designed to be given via *staff appraisal*. These staff appraisal systems involved staff members more and the process looked at behaviour in the job and often personality traits as well. The staff member was usually present and allowed to comment on the manager's views but not expected to contribute much. There was an emphasis on **appraising** past performance. The salary review was disconnected from the process.

The 1980s saw a much more participative style. By now the process was usually called *performance review*. It had become more open and outcome-focused. The employee was expected to prepare and reflect beforehand, ask questions and respond to the manager. The emphasis was on jointly **reviewing** past performance and considering **future performance**. Development plans were introduced as an important part of the process.

Currently in the 1990s the feedback process is even more open and is now frequently driven and owned by the employee. It has an emphasis on **counselling**, self-appraisal and self-development. The process is often labelled *performance management* and:

- is focused on important competencies required in the job, or outcomes required by the organization
- identifies the key performance drivers required to achieve organizational success
- is forward-looking with an emphasis on goals
- recognizes past successes and often rewards them with a performance bonus
- focuses on development and ongoing feedback from peers, subordinates and suppliers as well.

YOU MAY NOW CONTINUE WITH THE NEXT FAST TRACK SECTION ON PAGE 43
OR MOVE TO THE SKILLBUILDER EXERCISE ON PAGES 36–37

Effective Feedback

Circle the six words you would use to describe effective feedback.

friendly
descriptive
specific
general
critical
supportive
positive
fuzzy
realistic
timely
constructive
judgemental
immediate
authoritarian
blaming
accurate

Now compare your choices with those given in Answer Box 3.1 on page 40.

SKILLBUILDER

Feedback Style

You can assess your feedback style by completing this audit.

Read the five statements in the left-hand column of the audit. For each statement, choose the response which you feel you would most probably make if you were giving feedback to that person. Be honest with yourself – there are no simple 'right answers'. You will find an explanation of your scores in Answer Box 3.2 on page 40.

Statement
A. David 'I've been successful at every job I've had and I intend to be successful here whatever it takes. I'm determined to really go places.'
B. Jane 'Getting a business degree has really helped me to develop into a professional manager. I feel confident I can perform as well as any manager in this outfit.'
C. Hugh 'I used to be very career-minded but, as I've got older, success at work has become less important to me. My family are what's really important.'
D. Patricia 'I thought I'd make lots of new friends in this new job. I've always had no trouble in creating a social life. I enjoy the work, but people here don't seem interested in getting to know you. It's very disheartening.'
E. Ted 'I'm telling you, the Chief Executive has really got it in for me. I got the blame for the whole of the debt collection problem. Now he's trying to imply I'm falling down on the job. I'm concerned it will affect my reputation..'

Response
1. Tell me how you came to think that. **2.** Why are you so ambitious? **3.** It seems to me as if holding that view might affect your judgement on occasions. **4.** That attitude won't help you to become effective in this organization.
1. Becoming a professional manager requires experience as well as education. **2.** Can you think of any problems you might have in this organization? **3.** Tell me how you might manage in situations in which you have no experience. **4.** Your drive and confidence might hinder your ability to work well in a team.
1. This organization requires people who know what they want from their career. **2.** Yes, it's apparent that you decided to focus on your family. Does that give you problems at work? **3.** That's interesting what do you think triggered that change? **4.** In this last year your performance appears to have been unaffected by this.
1. I'd be interested to know how you go about making friends. **2.** Can you describe how that makes you feel at work? **3.** It's important to keep making a positive effort. **4.** On balance you appear to have managed pretty well.
1. You need to ensure it doesn't affect your performance. **2.** That's just one situation. Can you describe any other situations that have concerned you? **3.** It appears you are managing your responsibilities well at the moment. **4.** How do you feel you should approach this difficulty?

The Results of Effective Feedback

Effective feedback has three positive outcomes.

- It builds confidence. People receive positive feedback enabling them to maximize their strengths.
- It builds competence. People receive constructive feedback enabling them to manage and minimize their performance weaknesses.
- It encourages contribution. The process of giving and receiving feedback is powerful communication offering people the opportunity to validate their contribution to their role and to the team.

Effective feedback is always considerate and fair. It should be based upon performance not personality. We all have different styles of communication. The effective styles of feedback are those that utilize two-way communication such as open questioning, descriptive statements and active listening.

ANSWER BOX 3.1

Effective Feedback

1. **Descriptive** rather than judgemental. Offer a description of what you saw and how it made you feel, rather than a judgement. For example, '*When you said that, the customer felt ignored*' not '*You are so insensitive to customers*'.
2. **Supportive** not authoritarian. Help people to identify for themselves how they can improve rather than tell them the solution. Ask questions rather than make statements.
3. **Positive** and **constructive**, particularly when you need to criticize someone's performance. Positive and constructive feedback is a genuine **gift**. It builds people up. It tells people how you want them to change. Destructive feedback demoralizes people and knocks them down.
4. **Specific** and **accurate**. Relate your feedback to specifics – don't waffle on about general feelings and impressions. For example, '*I don't like the way you responded to that customer complaint*' not '*I don't like your attitude*'.
5. **Realistic**. Observe everyone's personal limits and don't give them impossible targets. Concentrate on behaviour that can be changed. For example, '*Why not make a list of what's gone wrong?*' not '*You're stupid*'.
6. **Timely**. Give feedback without delay – the earlier it is given the more helpful it is likely to be. Choose an appropriate place and give it in an unhurried manner.

ANSWER BOX 3.2

Feedback Style – Scoring

On the following table circle the option you selected for each situation on pages 36–37.

Statement	Response			
	Assessing	*Appraising*	*Reviewing*	*Counselling*
A	4	3	2	1
B	1	4	2	3
C	1	4	2	3
D	3	4	1	2
E	1	3	2	4

How many did you circle in each vertical column?

Carl Rogers in his research on face-to-face communication between managers and employees identified that managers tend to have habitual fixed ways of responding to subordinates. We therefore tend to overuse and underuse behaviours.

- Which categories of behaviour do you overuse?
- Which categories do you underuse?

There are no right ways of reviewing, but there are appropriate ways of reviewing for both the individual involved and the organization they work for.

UNIT 4 Managing Regular Feedback

In this unit we consider how to:

- **obtain helpful performance feedback from colleagues both informally and with the aid of a simple system**
- **communicate with, and brief, team members on performance issues**
- **handle everyday performance problems**
- **find opportunities and develop skills for delivering praise.**

Giving and receiving feedback from your team members can help you to:

- identify and deal with performance issues without delay
- harvest new ideas and issues you might never otherwise hear about
- maintain a 'temperature check' on team morale
- involve and motivate people
- build openness and trust
- make better decisions and set realistic goals.

Getting Feedback from Teams

It is important that your team is able to give feedback to you in a constructive way. To help them do this you could develop an Upward Team Feedback Sheet like the one shown below. Before you meet with them ask them to fill in their important observations and feelings under the specific headings. You will find that a system like this will help you to identify all the issues, feelings and grumbles you may not otherwise hear about. It will help your team to express them as issues, not just as moans.

Sound idea! Richer Sounds – one hi-fi retailer gives his staff a fiver once a month to go to the pub to think up ideas to make the company even better.

This Upward Team Feedback Sheet could slot into diaries or work planners or be used as a poster for a noticeboard, to be filled in as people think of things.

UPWARD TEAM FEEDBACK SHEET

Completed by	**For**
Date	**Place**
• Current issues to do with *resources and equipment* are:	Good news on resources and equipment is:
• Current issues to do with *goals and projects* are:	Good news on goals and projects working well are:
• Current issues to do with *communication* are:	Communications are working well in:
• Current issues to do with *feelings* are:	We're feeling good about:

YOU MAY NOW CONTINUE WITH THE NEXT FAST TRACK SECTION ON PAGE 44
OR MOVE TO THE SKILLBUILDER EXERCISE ON PAGE 49

Giving Feedback to Teams

Effective performance feedback leads to action and action leads to results – goals achieved, deadlines met, projects accomplished. Here are some tips for getting better at giving feedback.

If teams don't respond positively to feedback they probably need more.

- Have lunch or a drink with team members occasionally.
- Use the opportunity to discuss how they're doing.
- Look for opportunities to compliment good performance however small.
- Give people the gift of time.
- Find unusual and creative ways to give feedback:
  - progress charts pinned up in unusual places – for example, on loo doors, in rest rooms and so on.
  - 'Good News' boards where you can record success
  - A 'Boasting' board where they can record successes
  - handwritten 'thank you' notes.
- Hold 'morning prayer' sessions or team talks to review current and future projects and goals. The briefing sheet on page 50 provides a possible agenda.
- Find ways to build regular feedback into everyday routines so that people keep up-to-date.
- Include 'Stop Press' items with the monthly wage slips and consider writing a simple team newsletter.
- 'Walk the talk' regularly so that you know at first hand what's happening in your department. You can't give genuine performance feedback based on hearsay.
- If an issue at work keeps a person from doing his or her best, work with them to overcome it.

CHECK!

Remember, when giving feedback:

- always be natural and sincere
- weaknesses are needs not failures
- concentrate on what is important.

YOU MAY NOW CONTINUE WITH THE NEXT FAST TRACK SECTION ON PAGE 45
OR MOVE TO THE SKILLBUILDER EXERCISE ON PAGE 50

Performance Problems

Your team's performance is your responsibility. There will be times when performance problems arise and you will need to be prepared to resolve them quickly. If someone's poor performance or behaviour is affecting morale:

- Act immediately to maintain your team's respect and confidence and before the problem becomes worse.
- Look for causes. Seek feedback from other team members.
- Talk to the poor performer in confidence.
- Be direct about the effect the individual's behaviour is having on the rest of the team.
- Let the person 'feel' how you feel.
- Do not allow the individual to indulge in self-pity. Resolve the issue quickly, involving him or her in the choice of action. Give your full support.

When you end a 'reprimand' with praise people remember their behaviour not yours.

Remember, feedback is information designed to change behaviour in a positive way. It is *not* meant to be a censure which is merely a means of offloading your own anger and telling others how they should be.

CHECK!

If an employee or colleague brings a problem to you or asks for advice, listen and question them to ensure complete understanding.

- Ask them what they would like you to do to help.
- State what you can and cannot do.
- Let them know when you will take the action you have proposed.
- Summarize your understanding and what you've agreed to do.
- Do it and take note of your action.

CHECK!

If you spot a performance problem:

- deal with it now before it becomes habitual
- be clear and honest about what you need to say
- state the problem – be specific but tactful
- use statements like 'I see', 'I feel' . . .
- focus on the facts and behaviour not the person – for example, 'It was wrong' *not* 'You were wrong'
- ask for a solution: 'What could we do about it?'
- don't hold the lapse against them
- end on a note of praise.

YOU MAY NOW CONTINUE WITH THE NEXT FAST TRACK SECTION ON PAGE 46
OR MOVE TO THE SKILLBUILDER EXERCISE ON PAGE 51

Praising Performance

'Tell people what they do well and they'll do even better.' Praise can be delivered in a number of ways and in different combinations – for example:

- directly from you to them in the form of a compliment or a 'thank you'
- indirectly, through a third party – by getting someone else to compliment an individual on their performance
- indirectly, by making sure that the praise can be overheard or read about by the deserving party – for instance, through a newsletter
- formally through a reward such as a certificate, prize or bonus.

Focus on the individual's strengths. This is their future performance.

THE SEVEN MOST IMPORTANT SKILLS FOR MAKING PRAISE MEMORABLE . . .

❖ Be specific – because it makes it real.

❖ Smile – because it makes it sincere.

❖ Use their name – because it makes it personal.

❖ Describe the efforts of success – because we all want to do worthwhile things.

❖ Thank the person – because it gratifies them.

❖ Don't rush your praise – because it should be absorbed slowly, like sunshine.

❖ Give praise only when it is deserved.

YOU MAY NOW CONTINUE WITH THE NEXT FAST TRACK SECTION ON PAGE 47
OR MOVE TO THE SKILLBUILDER EXERCISE ON PAGE 52

Performance Feedback from Colleagues

Conventional performance review systems which may involve self-appraisal do not always give a complete picture. What about the views of the people you manage?

On the chart below, try identifying the important people, other than your manager, from whom you might obtain feedback.

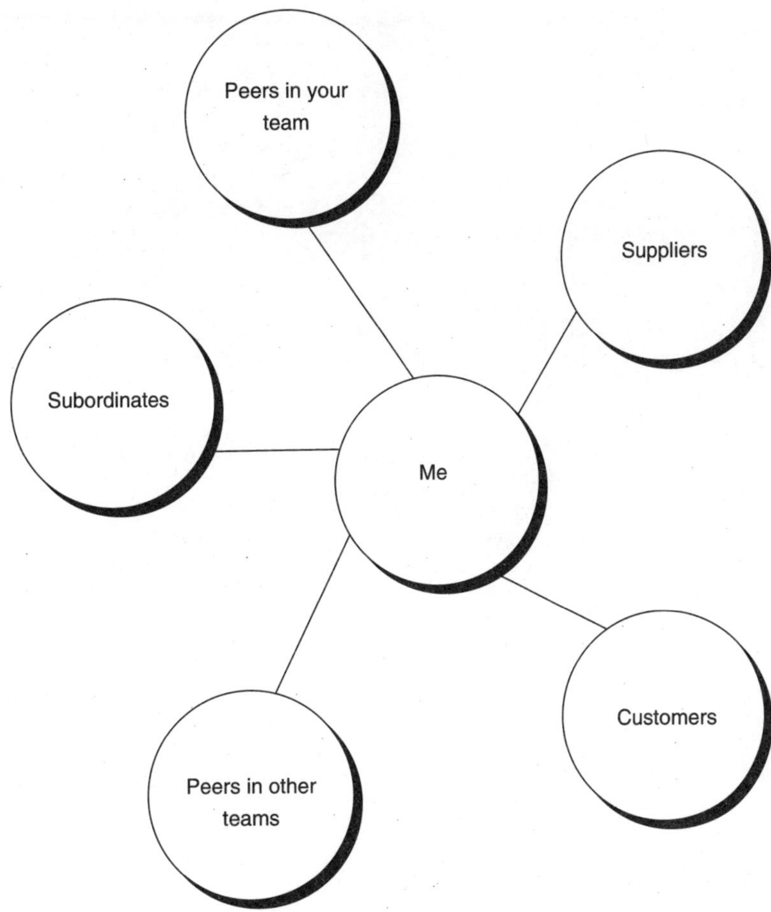

Consider asking them such questions as:

- What must I do to work well with you?
- What should I do?
- What could I do?

YOU MAY NOW CONTINUE WITH THE NEXT FAST TRACK SECTION ON PAGE 61
OR MOVE TO THE SKILLBUILDER EXERCISE ON PAGES 53–56

Getting Feedback from Teams

This first activity can be used as an informal team appraisal. It not only gives people the opportunity to explore others views of their performance but also encourages them to give and receive feedback in a constructive and supportive way.

- Sit down with one or several important team members.
- Take three pieces of paper each.
- On one of them write down all the things you'd like the other(s) to **do more of**.
- On another, write down the things you would like them to **do less of**.
- On the third, write down the things you want them to continue to **do just the same**.

Then exchange pieces of paper and discuss. Start with the third piece – it's a positive 'thank you' for what the team is doing. The other two contain some practical advice which you could use to negotiate team improvements!

This second activity can be used by:

- your team members to give you feedback
- by you to give them feedback or
- by team members to give each other feedback.

Circle any six words that describe the workstyle of . . . . (a member of your team)

Note that all the words are positive. It's the combination that people choose that provides you with insights.

tolerant supportive accurate
quick to react efficient dependent
persuasive reliable loyal
open logical honest assertive confident calm
decisive careful consistent attentive
authoritative demanding enthusiastic
approachable caring
sociable cautious comforting
sympathetic professional
ambitious emotional patient independent

Giving Feedback to Teams

You could use this team briefing sheet with the upward team feedback sheet described earlier. By giving you a clear agenda, it will help to bring focus and order to your information briefings.

TEAM BRIEFING	
Given by	**For**
Date	**Place**
RESOURCES AND EQUIPMENT	
Company issues	Department issues
GOALS AND PROJECTS	
Company issues	Department issues
COMMUNICATIONS AND EVENTS	
Company issues	Department issues

SKILLBUILDER

Performance Problems

Understanding how the person or people concerned feel about an issue, complaint or problem is an important part of giving feedback, particularly if you have to correct a performance problem.

Describe a current performance issue at work which is causing friction between teams, departments or individuals. Chart what you or the other person or people feel is:

- important to them about the issue
- unimportant to them about the issue
- liable to cause problems.

Now look at it through the eyes of the other person or people. What do you think he/she/they would feel?

My (our) view of the issue:	**What's important:**
What's unimportant:	**What could cause problems:**

Your team member's view:	**What he/she/they feel is important:**
What he/she/they feel is unimportant:	**What he/she/they feel could cause problems:**

SKILLBUILDER

Praising Performance

An effective way of praising performance is to put up a 'Good News' board in an employee area. This could be a Nobo board on which managers can record employees' special achievements, such as:

- clearing a backlog of work
- winning a departmental sports event
- managing an assignment with staff shortages
- winning compliments from customers on colleagues.

Update this news frequently. It should function as a wall newspaper and should have only one rule – good news only. You might also wish to put up a graffiti board on which colleagues could record their moans.

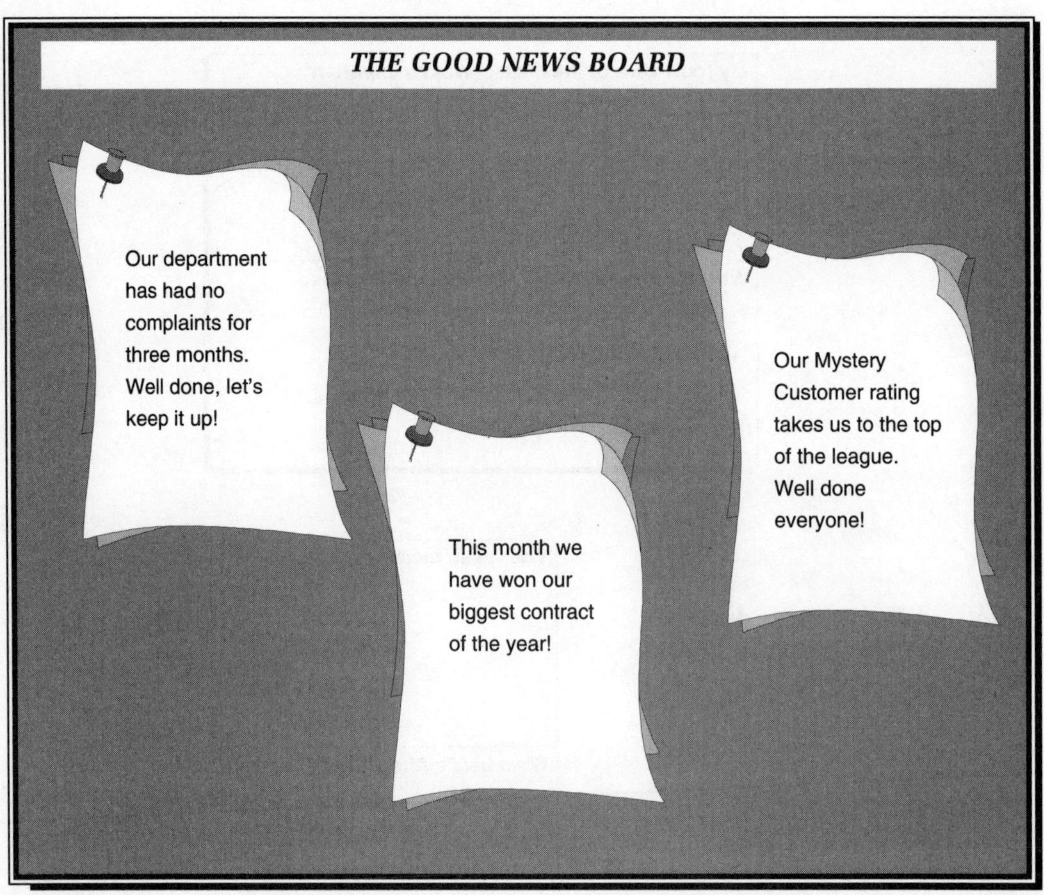

Performance Feedback from Colleagues

This upward feedback activity is designed for managers and supervisors who would like to know how their team rate their performance. Even though it may not be part of a formal system, the information gained will be extremely useful.

DISTRIBUTING THE QUESTIONNAIRE

The questionnaire on the following page should be completed anonymously by up to five or six subordinates or peers.

1. Fill in your name at the top of each questionnaire and distribute them. Stress that each respondent will remain anonymous and that you merely want some honest feedback on your performance.
2. Ask them to return the questionnaire to you or a third party by a certain date.

ANALYSING THE RESULTS

1. Make OHP transparencies of the performance profile (one for each questionnaire as in the example on page 56). Fill in each segment according to the score as in the example below.
2. Use a separate transparency to collect the information from each questionnaire. Block in the segments as follows: for Q1, the team member scored you B; for Q2, A and for Q3, C, and for Q4, B and so on. 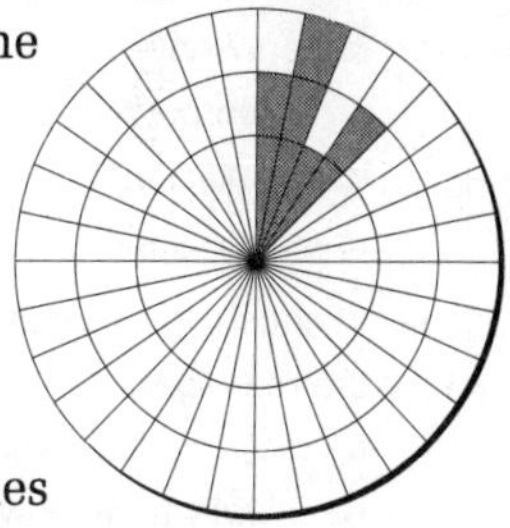
3. When complete, lay all the transparencies on top of each other to see if you have any performance shortfalls. For example:

   - Are there any segments where nobody gave you an A?
   - Did different people have very different views of your performance? If so, why do you think this is?

4. Make a list of your strengths and another list of factors which you feel are within your power to improve.
5. Write to each participant thanking them and telling them what action you will be taking.

SKILLBUILDER

COLLEAGUE PERFORMANCE FEEDBACK QUESTIONNAIRE

Name of Manager ....

Circle the response that you find best describes the named manager.

Performance and Productivity

1. When the manager's department achieves a high level of performance he/she usually:
   a. gives credit to those who did the work
   b. gives credit to the team as a whole
   c. takes credit for others' success

2. The manager, in setting goals for the team or myself:
   a. sets stretching but achievable goals
   b. sets goals which are too difficult to achieve
   c. is not clear about the goals

3. The manager, in maintaining standards:
   a. often seeks to improve them
   b. is satisfied with existing standards
   c. rarely refers to standards

4. The manager:
   a. is most concerned that I/we perform work that produces quality results
   b. is most concerned that I/we perform work that produces quick results
   c. is not concerned with the quality of my/our work

5. The manager's knowledge of the work being undertaken:
   a. is thorough and detailed
   b. is sufficient
   c. is adequate

6. In choosing between the urgent and important, the manager:
   a. distinguishes well between the two
   b. usually tends towards the urgent
   c. doesn't appear to know the difference between the two

7. The manager performs tasks:
   a. almost always well
   b. sometimes poorly and sometimes well
   c. almost always poorly

8. The manager achieves tasks:
   a. often ahead of time
   b. usually on time
   c. seldom on time

Procedures and Systems

9. In terms of equal opportunities, the manager:
   a. isn't biased and gives equal opportunity to everyone
   b. denies being biased but doesn't give equal opportunity to everyone
   c. gives obvious preference to certain people

10. The manager's knowledge and use of the financial systems:
   a. are excellent
   b. are competent
   c. require development

11. The manager develops and manages our admin systems:
   a. very professionally
   b. competently
   c. inadequately

12. The manager has developed and/or uses procedures for training and developing the team:
   a. very professionally
   b. competently
   c. inadequately

13. The manager plans the work of the department:
   a. very professionally
   b. competently
   c. inadequately

14. The manager schedules and organizes work:
   a. very professionally
   b. competently
   c. inadequately

15. The manager has developed and uses effective written communication systems:
   a. in all areas
   b. in some areas
   c. There are no communication systems or procedures

16. The manager holds effective team/departmental meetings:
   a. regularly
   b. occasionally
   c. hardly ever

People Skills

17. The manager is:

- **a.** usually fair
- **b.** occasionally unfair
- **c.** often unfair

18. The manager conveys to our team feelings of:

- **a.** security
- **b.** indifference
- **c.** fear and insecurity

19. When dealing with people serving our department, the manager treats them with:

- **a.** respect and kindness
- **b.** a professional manner
- **c.** a lack of consideration

20. The manager motivates me:

- **a.** very well
- **b.** adequately
- C not at all

21. The manager involves and consults me:

- **a.** on all appropriate matters
- **b.** on most appropriate matters
- **c.** seldom

22. In a crisis, the manager:

- **a.** gets the best from our team
- **b.** doesn't seem to affect the team
- **c.** adversely affects the team's performance

23. The manager creates an environment:

- **a.** that promotes creative and innovative ideas for selling our services
- **b.** that is neutral to creative and innovative ideas for selling our services
- **c.** that blocks creative and innovative ideas for selling our services

24. As far as the team is concerned, the manager:

- **a.** almost always chooses the right people
- **b.** usually chooses the right people
- **c.** seldom seems to choose the right people

Personal Qualities

25. The manager:

- **a** asks for constructive feedback
- **b** welcomes constructive feedback
- **c** seldom invites constructive feedback

26. The manager is:

- **a** mostly relaxed and friendly
- **b** usually relaxed and friendly
- **c** often tense and aggressive

27. The manager treats his/her subordinates:

- **a** almost always fairly and with respect
- **b** usually fairly and with respect
- **c** occasionally unfairly and without respect

28. The manager:

- **a** is usually creative and innovative
- **b** can be creative and innovative
- **c** resists new ideas

29. The manager:

- **a** is an exceptionally good listener
- **b** is a good listener
- **c** often interrupts and displays poor listening skills

30. The manager:

- **a** almost always considers other people's views
- **b** usually considers other people's views
- **c** rarely seems to consider the views of others

31. The manager is:

- **a** very trustworthy
- **b** usually trustworthy
- **c** untrustworthy

32. The manager represents the company:

- **a** well, leading people to trust and respect it
- **b** professionally and competently
- **c** poorly, creating concern about it

Adapted from 'Seen from below', a performance feedback questionnaire in *Maverick!* by Ricardo Semler (Century)

Performance Profile for Colleague Feedback

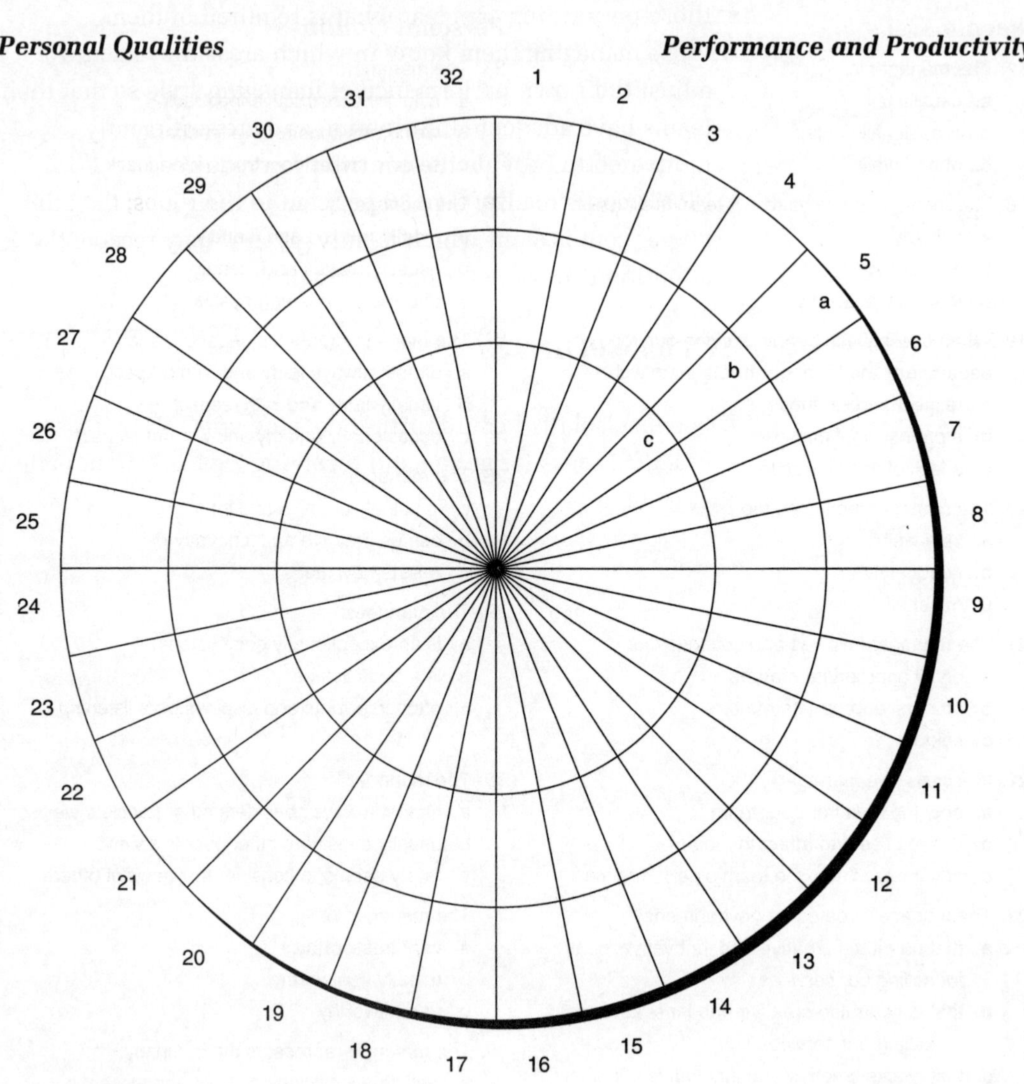

SKILLBUILDER

Managing Team Feedback

Giving and receiving feedback from teams makes sure that:

- those performing are clear what is required of them
- those managing them know in which areas they should adjust their own performance or managing style so that their teams have adequate information and are sufficiently motivated to provide the contribution required.
- Most people readily give 80 per cent to their jobs; the other 20 per cent is a gift which is only given if they receive the attention necessary for producing peak performance.

ACTION POINTS

- Feedback skills I could further develop are . . .
- Practical ideas for giving and receiving feedback from people at work are . . .

UNIT 5 Managing a Formal Review

In this unit you will develop a systematic approach to conducting a performance review discussion. The approach utilizes a seven-step framework with which you can manage and record the process of the performance review.

This seven-step framework to planning and conducting a performance review discussion is as follows.

- Jointly prepare for the discussion.
- Reflect on past performance.
- Explore past performance.
- Acknowledge and reward success.
- Explore problem areas.
- Develop a future action plan.
- Summarize and record the discussion.

In this unit you will also explore the important review skills of:

- building rapport through using the right questions and statements
- acknowledging success
- exploring problem areas
- developing an action plan.

Formal performance reviews generally take place annually and should ideally link to the business cycle. Staff can then understand what the business is trying to achieve in the next year and make a clear connection between business goals and their own performance targets. They can also make a clear connection between new learning, the skills required and their own training and development.

Step 1: Jointly Prepare for the Discussion

Performance should be reviewed and feedback given in a structured and objective way. To achieve this, organizations often have a formal review system which identifies the topics to discuss. These are generally based on what the organization is trying to achieve through the combined efforts of the individuals who work for it.

A performance review discussion should bring no surprises.

If you do not have a formal performance review system against which to review, develop your own performance agenda.

- Reflect on the individual's past performance, identifying important landmarks to which they contributed during the year.
- Explore the individual's past performance – what they did well, what adequately and what they learnt.
- Acknowledge and reward the success achieved by the individual. Highlight the difference their contribution made.
- Explore problem areas. With hindsight what do they and you think could have been done differently. What can be learned?
- Develop an action plan. Build for the future so the individual knows *where* and *how* to contribute and what to learn.
- Summarize and record your discussion. A summary confirms understanding and recording it provides a useful basis for the next review.

Develop your agenda with the person you will be reviewing up to a week in advance of the discussion. This will give both you and them an opportunity to plan for it.

YOU MAY NOW CONTINUE WITH THE NEXT FAST TRACK SECTION ON PAGE 62
OR MOVE TO THE SKILLBUILDER EXERCISE ON PAGE 71

Step 2: Reflect on Past Performance

Active listening teases out the meaning and the feeling in what someone else is saying.

Effective review involves looking back at the goals you agreed and assessing the success of the individual's performance. You then need to look ahead and set new goals which will help you frame the performance picture for the next period. The key skill when reflecting on past performance is to **listen actively** to what the person says.

Useful questions which will encourage the other person to talk and think about the past are:

- How have you found the last . . . months?
- What have you particularly enjoyed?
- What have you felt particularly proud of?
- What have you found difficult/challenging?

If you listen actively the other person will have the opportunity to express their thoughts.

ACTIVE LISTENING SKILLS

1. Know when to be silent.
   - Don't interrupt or finish others' sentences.
   - Don't say what you think until you know how others feel.

2. Don't make judgements.
   - Say 'That's interesting' rather than 'Yes, but'.

3. Summarize the main points.
   - The other person will be flattered to hear you summarizing what they have said. It will also help you understand and remember the key points.

4. Listen with your body.
   - We listen with our eyes as much as our ears, so watch people.
   - Use open gestures. They help you listen.

5. Listen for feelings as well as facts.
   - Use phrases like 'So what you mean is . . .' or 'So you are feeling . . .'

YOU MAY NOW CONTINUE WITH THE NEXT FAST TRACK SECTION ON PAGE 63
OR MOVE TO THE SKILLBUILDER EXERCISE ON PAGE 72

Step 3: Explore Past Performance

Having allowed the other person to reflect on their past performance, you will want to explore some specific areas of past performance. The key skill here is to **ask questions**.

Questions and statements

Building rapport with others and exploring the past is like moving along an arrowhead of questioning, which becomes sharper and more penetrating as you receive honest answers and therefore establish trust.

1. Open up encounters with contact questions.	*'I see that you spent time on . . .'*	These questions signal an interest in the other person.
2. Move on to general questions.	*'Tell me about . . .'* *'How have you found the last year?'*	These questions give the subject context.
3. Seek people's opinions.	*'How important do you think . . . was?'* *'What did you think about . . . ?*	These questions open up topics for discussion.
4. Probe people's opinions.	*'You said you found that project difficult. Tell me why.'*	These questions ask people to contribute facts and feelings to the discussion.
5. Pinpoint issues with closed questions.	*'Are you concerned about the present situation?'* *'Did you find the budget difficult to work with?'*	These questions isolate problems and opportunities to concentrate on.

Skilful questioners will usually start with contact questions and proceed through to the sharp end as they receive positive non-verbal cues from the other person, such as:

Deal with facts, not feelings. Feelings raise the temperature. Facts lower it.

- leaning forward signalling they are interested and keen
- an open posture demonstrates that they are at ease
- smiling while making direct eye contact which shows liking, trust and agreement
- head nodding – this is not only a sign of agreement but also of belief in what they're saying. Slow nods are the most positive. They signal agreement. Rapid head nods show impatience and a desire to move on or interrupt the other person.

Ask effective questions. Use a balance of these four types of questions to help you pace the direction and flow of your discussion.

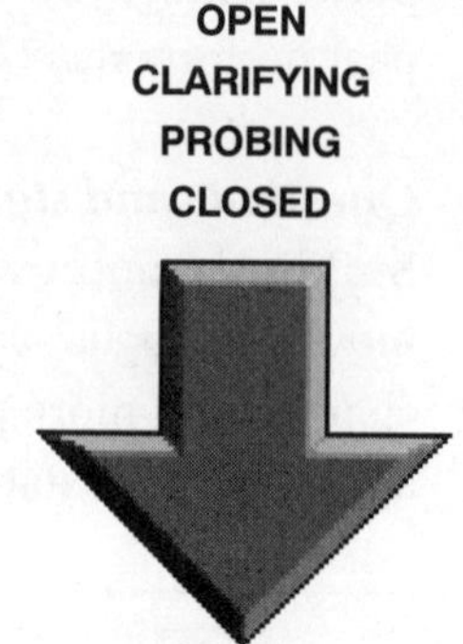

Open questions generate dialogue. Closed questions nail down specific facts.

1. Ask open questions (who?, what?, where?, how?) to:
- encourage the person to talk freely (particularly at the beginning)
- put the other person at their ease
- establish facts and opinions.

Avoid the 'why?' question – it can sound aggressive.

Example: *'What are you particularly pleased about'* rather than *'Why are you pleased?'*

2. Ask clarifying questions to:
- review what has been said
- check understanding and give the other person the opportunity to correct something
- reassure the other person that you understand.

Example: *'What does that mean to you?'*

3. Ask probing questions to:
- explore a point in more detail
- focus on detail.

Example: *'You'd expect to see the level of complaints dropping but that hasn't happened. Can you explain this?'*

4. Ask closed questions to:
- control the discussion
- confirm facts
- test agreement.

Example: *'Are we agreed that we will . . .?'*

YOU MAY NOW CONTINUE WITH THE NEXT FAST TRACK SECTION ON PAGE 65
OR MOVE TO THE SKILLBUILDER EXERCISE ON PAGES 73–74

Step 4: Acknowledge and Reward Success

Having reviewed past performance you are now in a position to provide positive feedback by acknowledging and rewarding successes. The key skill here is to **give genuine and sincere praise**.

When reviewing someone's performance, always start with praise. Make it specific, not general. Being recognized for an achievement is every bit as important as being praised.

There are two additional reasons why praise is such a powerful motivator.

- If you tell people what they've done well they will do even better.
- Praise improves people's hearing. In other words, they are much more likely to be objective about their performance if they feel that someone is being objective and fair about them.

As in informal feedback, the five important principles for making praise memorable are as follows:

- Be specific – because it makes it real.
- Smile – because it makes it sincere.
- Use their name – because it makes it personal.
- Describe the effects of the success – because we all want to do worthwhile things.
- Thank the person – because it gratifies them.

YOU MAY NOW CONTINUE WITH THE NEXT FAST TRACK SECTION ON PAGE 66
OR MOVE TO THE SKILLBUILDER EXERCISE ON PAGE 75

Step 5: Explore Problem Areas

Once you have dealt with success, you can move on to review areas of difficulty. The key skill here is to keep your feedback **constructive and non-judgemental**. Most people are wary about tackling difficult issues and their unease often leads to a failure to confront the issue at all. The following are guidelines for exploring problem areas.

Problems are usually learning needs.

1. Make your feedback constructive, by:

- asking questions before making statements
- offering a specific description of what you know or saw and how you feel, rather than a judgement – for example, *'The way you behaved towards the new supplier led to complaints from your colleagues'*
- concentrating on behaviour which can be changed.

2. When faced with disagreement:

- respond in a non-reactive way – don't try to convince, reason or give additional information
- don't be personal and remain objective – for example, *'As you know, I feel differently about this issue . . .'*
- if you are wrong in your interpretation of the facts, admit it.

3. When receiving negative feedback:

- respond rather than react. If it is information about past behaviour, use it to improve – for example, *'I can see now why you felt I was getting at you. In future I'll . . .'*
- ask questions and request examples in a neutral manner
- thank people regardless
- tell people how it makes you feel – for example, concerned, willing to change and so on.

YOU MAY NOW CONTINUE WITH THE NEXT FAST TRACK SECTION ON PAGE 67
OR MOVE TO THE SKILLBUILDER EXERCISE ON PAGE 76

Step 6: Develop a Future Action Plan

The process of reviewing performance and providing feedback must be forward – as well as backward-looking. Developing a plan for the future is, therefore, an essential part of the review process. In developing the future, you should:

Devote at least half of the discussion to the future and don't make promises you can't keep!

- meet the development needs and interests of the other person
- contribute to meeting the needs of the organization.

These should be parallel outcomes and you should make sure that you jointly describe goals that provide the other person with a clear performance plan for the next period and identify the skill gaps that might cause difficulties in accomplishing it.

1. You will need to identify performance goals that enable the other person **to contribute**. These can be expressed as discrete tasks or projects, such as:

   - *to organize the office move*
   - *to cut department costs by 10 per cent*

   Any such tasks should be accompanied by time and money budgets.

2. You will also need to identify goals that enable the other person **to build competence – personal development goals**. These will then enable the person to achieve the level of contribution required and can be expressed as development needs, such as:

   - *to become competent in the use of the Windows 95 software package.*

YOU MAY NOW CONTINUE WITH THE NEXT FAST TRACK SECTION ON PAGE 68
OR MOVE TO THE SKILLBUILDER EXERCISE ON PAGE 77

FAST TRACK

Step 7: Summarize and Record the Discussion

It is important to summarize the review discussion and to record the important decisions made, and the commitments the person can expect from you to help them achieve their goals.

- Discuss and agree the overall performance achieved and also summarize goals defined for the forthcoming period.
- Describe what support and help you will be able to provide in the next period, and in which specific areas.

In a changing work environment, we need to encourage people to think of their employability not just their employment.

A performance review frames the performance picture. In order to paint the picture for the next period you will need to confirm the kind and frequency of feedback that the individual would appreciate. This will enable you to monitor progress and confirm your commitment to them.

YOU MAY NOW CONTINUE WITH THE NEXT FAST TRACK SECTION ON PAGE 69
OR MOVE TO THE SKILLBUILDER EXERCISE ON PAGE 78

Follow Up

A formal performance review is an important discussion for both parties. It consolidates the performance of the previous period and enables you to contract jointly for responsibilities in the next performance period.

The person being reviewed should contract to:

- self-develop in identified areas
- take responsibility for achieving identified performance goals.

The reviewer should contract to:

- provide coaching support and help as appropriate
- empower and authorize the other person to achieve the stated goals
- regularly monitor and follow up the other person.

The performance review is like a 12 000 mile service on your car. You still need to maintain performance in between by making regular checks.

Don't forget to confirm agreements and record all documentation. Either file it or send it to appropriate departments, such as Personnel.

YOU MAY NOW CONTINUE WITH THE NEXT FAST TRACK SECTION ON PAGE 89
OR MOVE TO THE SKILLBUILDER EXERCISE ON PAGE 79

Plan the Performance Review Discussion

You need to develop an agreed agenda for the discussion. This forms Step 1 of the seven-step framework set out below. This framework will provide the discussion with focus. The framework will help you to:

- get the review discussion started
- review performance
- look to the future
- conclude the discussion.

The questions in each section will provide you with useful prompts as you move through the discussion.

1

Jointly Prepare for the Discussion

- The format for the meeting
- The topics to discuss
- Start on a positive note
- State the aims of the review
- Explain that you will summarize the main points discussed in note form

2

Reflect on Past Performance

- How have you found the last year?

3

Explore Past Performance

- Let's take . . . first and explore that
- What are you particularly pleased with?
- What do you feel could have been done better?
- What did you learn?

4

Acknowledge and Reward Success

- I was particularly pleased with how you . . .
- Your contribution here means that we . . .

5

Explore Problem Areas

- In what specific areas could you have improved the results?
- With hindsight what do you now feel?

6

Develop an Action Plan

- Where would you like to focus?
- What does the organization/department need from you?
- What changes will be happening?
- What development, coaching, training could help?

7

Summarize and Record the Discussion

- Summarize key points and all discussions

Reflect on Past Performance

Check to see whether you display any of these symptoms of poor listening and apply appropriate remedies.

Symptom	Remedy
I ask a question but switch off before I'm given the full reply.	Search for hidden information of value to you. Take notes to help you concentrate. Maintain eye contact, lean forward and react to what is being said by nodding, saying 'Yes'/'No' and so on.
I pick up on facts and react to these.	Look behind the facts for the concepts or ideas that lie behind them.
I have other things on my mind that stop me concentrating.	Leave other problems behind. Focus completely on the other person to help you consider 'What's next?' or 'What if?'.
I get tired and then my concentration slips.	Listening *is* tiring. You need to train to be a good listener. Set goals for the meeting and concentrate on achieving these.
I'm too busy thinking about how I'm going to reply to listen.	Slow down. Use silence to gather your thoughts so that you can concentrate when the other person is talking.
I'm too nervous to listen properly.	Have a set of questions prepared in advance. Take it slowly and use silence to get the other person to talk.

SKILLBUILDER

For each of the following statements identify an appropriate 'active listening' response. See Answer Box 5.1 on page 82 for example answers.

'I never seem to be given interesting tasks to do.'

____

'When I joined the organization I thought I'd achieve a good position. I've been here for four years and I'm still in the same job.'

____

'I really enjoy my job. The extra responsibility's been a challenge.'

____

Explore Past Performance

Think of some review questions you might ask that could give you access to boxes B, C and D.

A Facts you are certain of . . .	B Facts you need to find out, eg How many customer complaints did we get last month
C Facts you know but don't fully understand, eg I know you gather customer complaints but please tell me how you do it.	**D** Facts you don't know anything about, eg I know nothing about the complaint handling part of your job. Please explain it.

We use statements to tell others what we already know. We use questions to confirm what we already know or to discover facts or explore feelings.

SKILLBUILDER

Now read each of the following questions to find out whether you recognize each type. Answers can be found in Answer Box 5.2 on page 82

Question	Open? Probing? Closed? Clarifying?
1. 'What do you enjoy most about your job?'	
2. 'Can you explain that further?'	
3. 'Is it a good idea to go ahead with this?'	
4. 'What I hear you say is that you want more challenge?'	
5. 'How did you deal with the situation?'	
6. 'Can you describe what you mean by that?'	
7. 'What do you consider have been your most important successes?'	

Questions help us to steer the conversation. If the other person seems intent on raising issues which are inappropriate, try guiding the conversation by asking a question like 'How does this issue relate to your performance?'.

Acknowledge and Reward Success

Make sure that the praise you give is memorable. Consider the person whom you are reviewing and plan how you will recognize their achievements. Improvements, however small, are always praiseworthy.

What will you praise?	
How will you make it specific?	
How will you describe the effects of the success?	
How will you thank them?	

Explore Problem Areas

Try to provide positive feedback alternatives to the statements below. Suggested answers are in Answer Box 5.3 on page 83.

Statements	Positive Alternatives
1. *'I didn't like your attitude in that project meeting.'* Be descriptive rather than judgemental.	
2. *'This is what we'll do.'* Be supportive not authoritarian.	
3. *'Jack, you've been very uncooperative lately.'* Be specific and accurate. Focus on performance not personality.	
4. *'I can't imagine why visitors seem to like you but they do.'* Be prepared to praise successes and improvements (however slight).	
5. *'I'm afraid liaison is your weakest area.'* Be positive and constructive – describe weaknesses as needs.	
6. *'You must be more assertive.'* Be realistic. Concentrate on behaviour that can be changed.	

SKILLBUILDER

Develop a Future Action Plan

Use the performance map below to summarize your jointly agreed action plan and to identify clear goals for:

- relevant contribution
- enhanced competence.

<table>
<tr><td>Name:</td><td>Date:</td></tr>
<tr><td colspan="2">The purpose of my job next year will be to . . .</td></tr>
<tr><td>Goals which will ensure that my contribution to the organization is relevant are . . .</td><td>Development goals which will help me enhance my competence are . . .</td></tr>
<tr><td>Don't forget to include measures of success, time, money, quantity, and so on.</td><td>Don't forget to include dates by which to achieve and methods for development such as self-development, coaching, on-job training, courses.</td></tr>
</table>

SKILLBUILDER

Summarize and Record the Discussion

The person you are reviewing should take ownership of the discussion. Asking you the following questions will:

- summarize the review
- describe the support they can expect from you in the future.

A SELF-SUMMARY	
Goals • How would you describe my performance last year? • What are the key goals I need to achieve this year, and how will I set about achieving them?	
Involvement and feedback • What can I expect from you, my manager, in terms of feedback, coaching, counselling, mentoring, advice and time?	
Feedback • What kind of feedback can I expect from you and my colleagues? • What kind of feedback are you willing to receive from me?	
Monitoring and training • What is the best way of tracking my progress, and the progress of my key goals and tasks?	

Remember your summary of the discussion should be fair and succinct.

- Use phrases such as 'We agreed,' 'We planned'.
- Use positive words such as 'development', 'opportunities', 'needs'.
- Note down the actions you have agreed to take to support the other person.
- Summarize the other person's career opportunities, if applicable.
- Make a summary of both viewpoints in case there are any areas of disagreement later.

Follow Up

Write down the actions you feel you should take immediately after the review and before the next formal review. Compare your checklist with Answer Box 5.4 on page 84.

What I must do immediately after the review	*What I must do before the next review*

SKILLBUILDER

Managing a Formal Review

When conducting a formal review discussion make sure that you cover the following points. Use the blank framework on the next page to help you with your next review discussion.

1. Get the review meeting started.

- Start on a positive note.
- State the aims of the review.
- Encourage the person to talk freely – ask general open questions first.
- Explain that you will summarize the main points discussed in note form.

2. Review performance.

- Encourage the person to self-appraise.
- Deal with one activity at a time.
- Recognize strengths and achievements.
- Discuss weaknesses as needs: explore reasons for underachievement; agree support and help.

3. Look to the future.

- Agree goals for each topic and record them so that they can serve as a basis for the next review.
- Identify, agree and record training and development needs.
- Emphasize what you will do to support the other person – for example, coaching, feedback, support.

4. Conclude the discussion.

- Summarize the discussion.
- Complete a written summary, ask the other person to make any final comments and sign them.
- Make no further additions without the other person's involvement.
- End on a positive note.

ACTION POINTS

Use this blank seven-step framework to help you prepare and manage the next performance review discussion you have.

THE SEVEN-STEP FRAMEWORK FOR REVIEWING PERFORMANCE

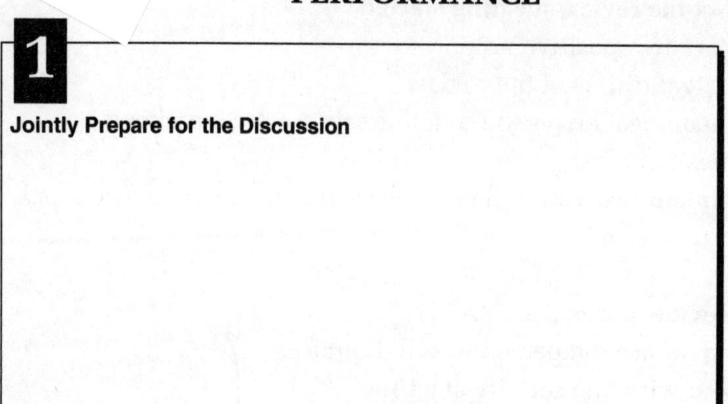

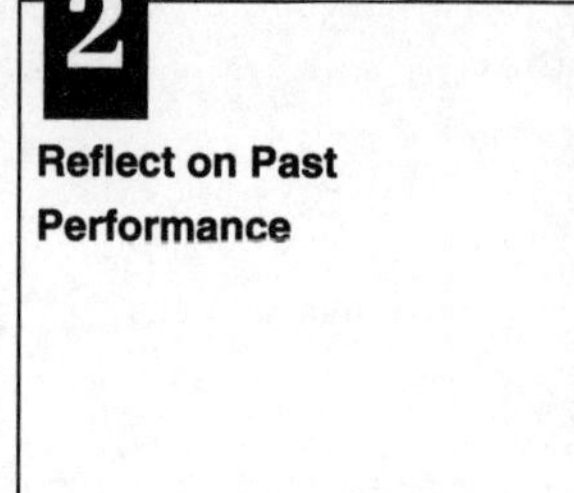

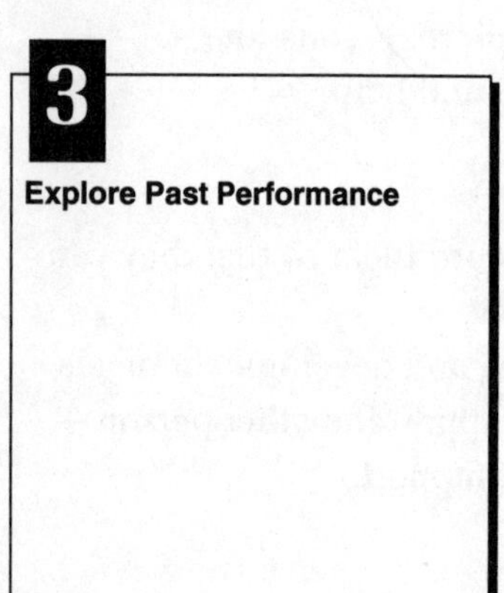

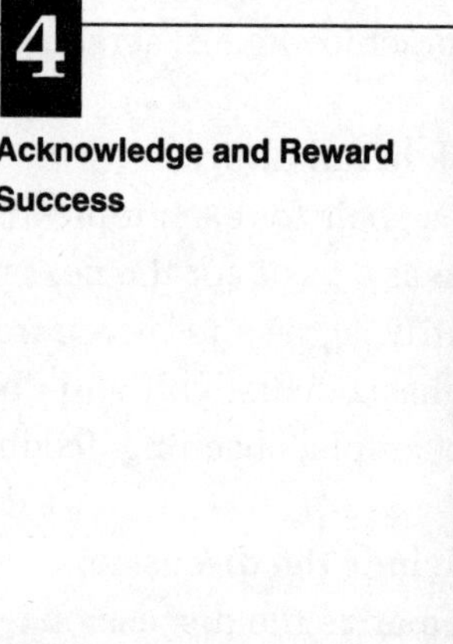

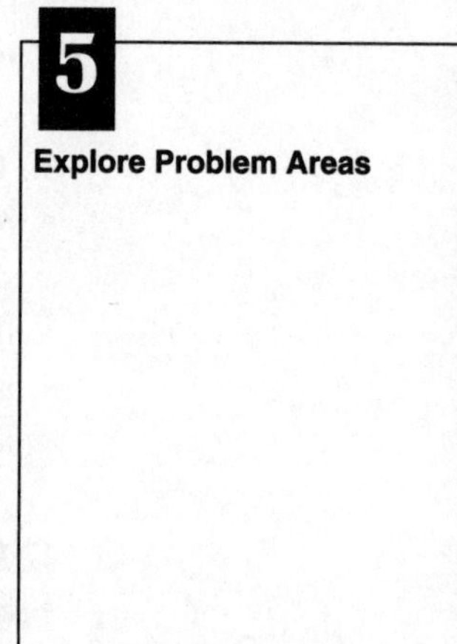

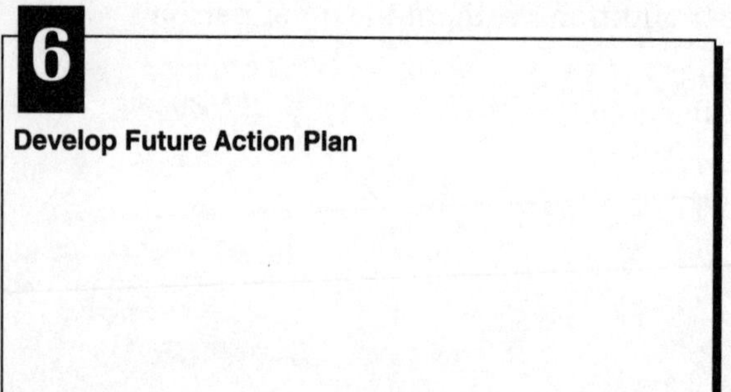

ANSWER BOX 5.1 ACTIVE LISTENING RESPONSES

Statement	Suggested Response
'I never seem to be given interesting tasks to do.'	'I'm sorry to hear that. Can you give me some examples of situations where you feel you've missed out?'
'When I joined the organization I thought I'd achieve a good position somewhere. I've been here for four years and I'm still in the same job.'	'Where would you have liked to be by now and what do you feel you would have needed to learn?'
'I really enjoy my job. The extra responsibility's been a challenge.'	'That's good to hear. Tell me about your extra responsibilities and how you are managing them.'

ANSWER BOX 5.2 TYPES OF QUESTIONS

1. Open
2. Probing
3. Closed
4. Clarifying
5. Open
6. Probing
7. Open

ANSWER BOX 5.3 EXPLORE PROBLEM AREAS: SUGGESTED ANSWERS

1. 'It would have been helpful if you could have contributed to that project meeting.'
2. 'What do you suggest that we could do?'
3. 'Jack. Things seem to have been difficult for you lately. Tell me about it.'
4. 'You are very sensitive in the way you handle visitors.'
5. 'I think your communication skills could be developed even more.'
6. 'We must help you learn to say 'no' to the demands of your colleagues sometimes.'

ANSWER BOX 5.4 FOLLOW UP

Immediately after the review

- Complete all documentation and ask the other person to confirm their agreement. Make no further changes without their approval.
- Distribute the documents to relevant people – for instance, to your manager, Personnel, the person you have reviewed.
- Follow up any outstanding issues immediately.
- Don't forget to critique how the review session went:
  - What did the other person think of it?
  - What have you learned from the experience?
  - How could you improve your skills for next time?

Before the next review

- Monitor and follow up the person's performance.
- Arrange informal review discussions occasionally – for example, to revise objectives and review training requirements.
- Provide for specific coaching as appropriate.

PART III Managing Coaching Assignments

The second half of this Workbook concerns winning commitment from your team-members; this will enable you to actively manage the performance of your staff and develop their jobs for them.

Using coaching as a means of involving others at work helps you facilitate their learning and at the same time delegate tasks, activities and authority. Coaching is a necessary activity within today's lean management teams for the following reasons:

- It empowers others.
- It develops others.
- It frees you from tasks that you are now familiar with and in which you have expertise.

Part III will show you how to actively manage the performance of people at work by giving you:

- quick access to the skills involved in coaching individuals and teams
- a seven-step framework for describing assignments and managing each coaching session
- insights and practical ideas with which to improve your management style.

UNIT 6 What is Coaching?

In this unit we consider:

- **what coaching is and the benefits it can bring both to you and your team**
- **your own coaching style**
- **how to choose a coaching assignment.**

If you ask most people what they understand by coaching their reply will usually include reference to sport. We are all familiar with the football and tennis coach. All the best teams and players have one so they must be important, but what do they actually do?

Coaching is providing a person or group with the **guidance**, **support** and **confidence** to enable them to enhance their performance **continuously.**

- **Guidance** enables someone to develop their skills and knowledge appropriately. Through skilful guidance a coach can also help another person develop useful insights into their work and their character.
- **Support** means being there *only* when you're needed.
- **Confidence** means believing in someone so that they can believe in themselves and perform successfully.
- **Continuously** means all the time! Coaching is not something which is turned on and off like a tap. Successful coaching depends on planning coaching assignments and developing supportive relationships over time.

Why Coach?

The simple answer to this question is to 'improve performance'. Today, a manager's success depends on the performance he or she can generate from others. Managing performance nowadays is based on managing the intelligence and commitment of people. It is no longer a matter of controlling 'hired hands'.

In modern organizations managers have greater responsibility but less control. They have greater responsibility because, in the flatter organizations, a manager can be responsible for 30 or 40 people – a far cry from the times of Max Weber, who coined the term 'bureaucracy' and reckoned that six or seven was the norm. Equally, managers have less control because wider access to information and an empowerment culture have expanded the organization's decision-making base to involve everyone – not just managers.

Managers therefore need a facilitative management style which is characterized by:

- cooperation
- trust and
- commitment.

These three characteristics lie at the heart of successful coaching. Your ability to coach those on whom your own performance depends is a key strategy for performance improvement.

Coach people to be better performers. Don't keep them confined; don't fear being challenged. Your talent is developing their talent.

Successful coaching always results in higher levels of:

- commitment
- competence and
- communication.

YOU MAY NOW CONTINUE WITH THE NEXT FAST TRACK SECTION ON PAGE 90
OR MOVE TO THE SKILLBUILDER EXERCISE ON PAGE 93

Identify your Coaching Style

There is no 'correct' coaching style. Each individual you coach will respond differently and you need to be flexible. The only rule, therefore, is to adopt a style that facilitates commitment and communication in the coaching assignment and that results in the improved competence of the individual.

In involving yourself with others and helping them to learn, you could:

- direct
- persuade
- coach
- counsel.

The key to successful coaching is knowing when to use the appropriate style not just the one with which you feel most comfortable.

So what do the four coaching styles actually entail?

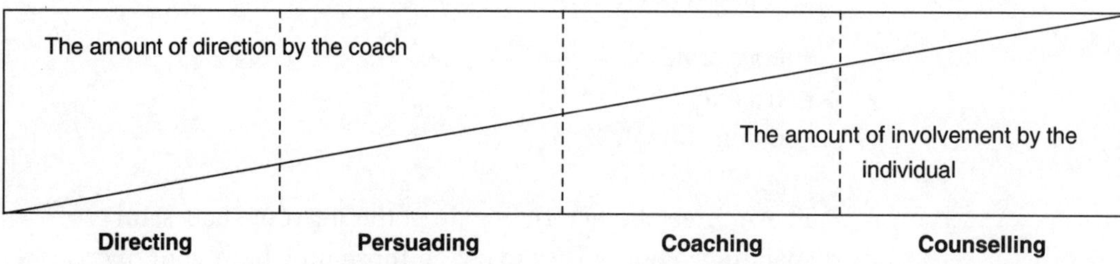

Mirrors or windows? A good coach acts like a window, enabling the other person to see new possibilities, not like a mirror reflecting back his or her current knowledge.

- **Directing**. A coach preferring to use this style wants to take control of the encounter. He or she would tell the person being coached what to do. They would be likely to use statements and make little or no use of questions. For example: 'You must assemble the instrument as I show you. . . .'
- **Persuading**. A coach using this style would adopt a salesperson's approach to the coaching session. He or she would make use of closed questions and persuasive statements. For example: 'This is the best way to assemble the instrument. Can you see the order I have followed?'
- **Coaching**. A coach using this style would ensure the coaching session was a learning opportunity. He or she would set clear goals and delegate action. He or she would

make use of open questions and would listen carefully and supportively to the person being coached.

For example: 'At the end of this session you will be able to demonstrate how this instrument is assembled. Can you suggest what the first steps might be?'

- **Counselling**. A coach using this style would try to encourage the person being coached to think through the solutions for themselves. They would not seek to guide but to listen, use reflective questions and paraphrase.

  For example: 'That's interesting, so you think the first steps you might take are . . .'

YOU MAY NOW CONTINUE WITH THE NEXT FAST TRACK SECTION ON PAGE 92
OR MOVE TO THE SKILLBUILDER EXERCISE ON PAGE 94

Choosing an Assignment

Coaching requires the manager to invest time in order to achieve long-term gain. The ideal coaching assignment is a project or task that you would like to delegate and that the other person would like to learn. The benefit to you will be saving of time in the long term. Many managers don't recognize coaching opportunities because they concentrate on achieving tasks, not on developing people. Where would you place yourself on the spectrum below?

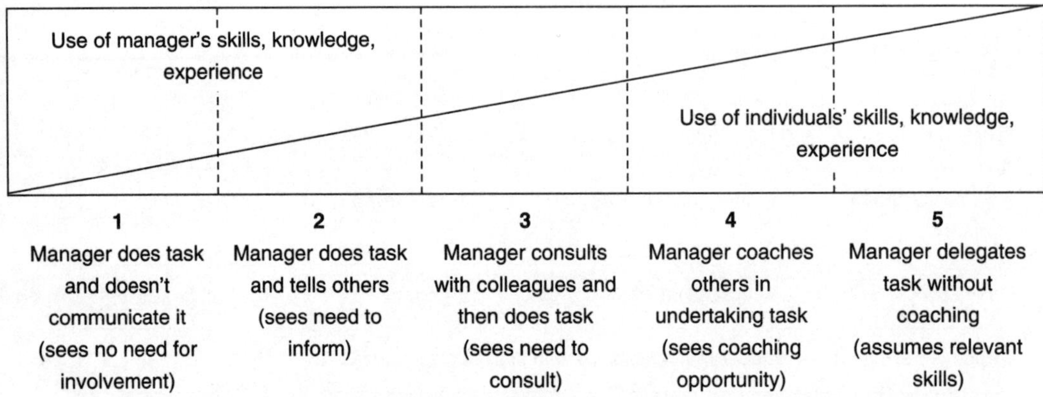

Looking at the coaching assignment from the other person's point of view, an assignment must:

- improve current competencies
- develop new competencies
- provide a 'hands-on' opportunity to carry out a significant, relevant task
- fit in with their long-term development plans.

The following skillbuilder will provide the other person with some useful insights into their own needs that might translate into coaching opportunities.

For coaching to be effective the person being coached must be:

- committed
- cooperative and
- trustworthy

as they will be given genuine responsibility for real work.

YOU MAY NOW CONTINUE WITH THE NEXT FAST TRACK SECTION ON PAGE 101
OR MOVE TO THE SKILLBUILDER EXERCISE ON PAGE 95

Why Coach?

Complete this short questionnaire to find out whether you have a coaching mindset. Rate the extent to which you agree or disagree with each statement by circling a number according to the following scale:

I strongly agree	1
I agree	2
I am indifferent	3
I disagree	4
I strongly disagree	5

Statement	Rating				
It would please me if some of my team were better than me at work-related tasks.	1	2	3	4	5
I think it's important for my team not to see me as always having the right answers.	1	2	3	4	5
I think people learn more effectively at work.	1	2	3	4	5
I need to develop more productive relationships with individuals in my team.	1	2	3	4	5
I have to be able to depend on individuals in my team to get the job done without referring to me.	1	2	3	4	5
I would rather be valued than needed by others.	1	2	3	4	5
I need team members who can define their own solutions to change.	1	2	3	4	5
I would rather develop existing employees than acquire extra staff.	1	2	3	4	5
I need team members who can provide different solutions to me.	1	2	3	4	5
Total					

If you scored 22 or less, you understand that coaching involves improving the performance of others, sharing your authority and knowledge and delegating action. You, like the best coaches, are willing to share your experience whilst helping others develop their own unique talents.

If you scored 23 or more you may need to consider whether your desire to control situations and people is hindering your ability to develop a modern, appropriate management style.

Identify your Coaching Style

This questionnaire will help you assess your coaching style. Complete each of the statements in the left-hand column of the table by selecting the option in the right-hand column that most closely reflects your own style. Be honest with yourself – there are no 'right answers'. You can identify your style(s) in Answer Box 6.1 on page 98.

Statement	Option
A. The best way to achieve things at work is to . . .	**1.** Tell others what's required and convince them to work to my plan. **2.** Design tasks that people can learn from at the same time as getting the job done. **3.** Have a clear idea of what's required and ensure my team members work to that. **4.** Let team members work it out for themselves and use me for support and help.
B. Delegating tasks at work means . . .	**1.** Being there to help others if and when required. **2.** Directing others as to exactly what's required so that they can get it done right. **3.** Describing necessary outcomes as assignments so that people can use their discretion and judgement in completing a task and learn something in the process. **4.** Encouraging people to accept responsibility by showing them how they will benefit from it.
C. Coaching others principally entails . . .	**1.** Telling others what to do. **2.** Persuading others what they must do. **3.** Supporting others in carrying out their own ideas. **4.** Guiding others to achieve the necessary outcomes.
D. Coaching others . . .	**1.** Is very demanding and takes up a lot of time. **2.** Requires control at the outset to define the boundaries, then leaving people to do it for themselves and reviewing outcomes at the end. **3.** Means that you often have to spend time influencing others to take on responsibilities which they may not have thought they were capable of. **4.** Means that you must keep your distance so that at all times people can develop their own ways of carrying out a task.
E. Coaching is . . .	**1.** Apprenticeship revisited and updated. **2.** Non-directive development. **3.** Delegation by influence. **4.** Directing others to correct performance.

Choosing an Assignment

Coaching yields **opportunities for delegation**. To find out how much opportunity there is to delegate tasks through coaching assignments, ask the other person to complete the assessment sheets below.

CURRENT LEARNING NEEDS ASSESSMENT

A self-development method for learning how to . . .

I could:

- speak to . . .
- read about . . .
- study an open-learning pack on . . .

A coaching method for learning how to . . .

I could:

- work alongside . . .
- do a coaching assignment with . . .

A course method for learning about . . .

I could do a specific course on . . .

MULTI-SKILLING OPPORTUNITIES

Relevant tasks in the organization that I could **learn** to perform are:

Changes in the organization in which I could become **involved** are:

Relevant skills needed by the organization in which I could improve my **competence** are:

New skills that I could **develop** are:

What is Coaching?

One of the successful outcomes of coaching is the opportunity for increased delegation. Consider the following questions:

- Have you any assignments or tasks that have now become routine?
- Would you like time to concentrate on new things?
- If you had to delegate three activities what would they be?

Now consider these questions:

- Is there someone who might do the task in a different way to you or take a bit more time but who could still achieve an acceptable level of performance?
- Is there someone who would benefit from doing the task in terms of their personal development?

If you can answer 'Yes' to any of these questions, you have identified an opportunity for gaining the key mutual benefit from coaching – *YOU DELEGATE, SOMEONE LEARNS!*

ACTION POINTS

- Suitable coaching assignments that I can identify are . . .
- Suitable people for coaching are . . .

ANSWER BOX 6.1 IDENTIFY YOUR COACHING STYLE

Use the following grid to assess your range of coaching styles according to the option you selected for each statement in the style check questionnaire on page 94.

Circle the option you chose for each statement.

Statement	Direct	Persuade	Coach	Counsel
A	3	1	2	4
B	2	4	3	1
C	1	2	4	3
D	1	3	2	4
E	4	3	1	2

If you have selected three in one category you have indicated that you feel comfortable using that style. When coaching, effective coaches use the styles in the following way:

- They **coach** 75 per cent of the time.
- They **persuade** 10 per cent of the time.
- They **counsel** 10 per cent of the time.
- They **direct** 5 per cent of the time.

Ask yourself these two questions:

- What is my preferred style – is it more directive or more involving?
- Does my style fit well with the culture of my organization?

UNIT 7 A Framework for Coaching

In this unit you will be able to develop a systematic approach to managing a coaching assignment at work. You will explore three effective coaching skills for

- **asking the right questions**
- **active listening**
- **paraphrasing and reflecting.**

You will also learn how to develop an effective action plan enabling your team member to assume responsibility in a planned manner.

The approach uses a seven-step framework with which you can manage and record each coaching session and form a coaching portfolio for each assignment. The whole coaching assignment can be tracked and managed with the completed seven-step framework.

The seven steps are as follows:

- Identify and jointly agree the topic.
- Identify the goals.
- Explore the current position.
- Explore the options.
- Develop an action plan.
- Give authority to act.
- Summarize the session.

Step 1: Identify and Jointly Agree the Topic

In establishing a coaching assignment it is essential that you both jointly agree a suitable topic. This will ensure you are both committed to it.

Suitable opportunities for coaching emerge in a number of ways: through reviewing performance; through seeking opportunities for delegation; through developing the team member's job or 'multi-skilling' them.

Coaching will provide you with opportunities to delegate and develop a person so that they are capable of developing their job and accepting increased responsibility.

The following skillbuilders help the person you are going to coach identify topics which could be delegated to them and then to jointly agree them.

First, find out how involved the other person considers they are with different tasks, and where there may be opportunities for coaching. Ask them to list six important current activities that your department or team are undertaking and to place a tick in the appropriate column.

The further their responses lie to the right of the table the more they will benefit from coaching.

JOB TASK	I do it on my own	I do it but tell my team or manager	I talk with my manager and then do it	I talk with my colleagues and then do it	I have to leave it to someone else	I am uninvolved

SUMMARY

Use the space below to identify suitable coaching topics you have identified.

Suitable topics/assignments for coaching are:

1.
2.
3.
4.
5.

YOU MAY NOW CONTINUE WITH THE NEXT FAST TRACK SECTION ON PAGE 102
OR MOVE TO THE SKILLBUILDER EXERCISE ON PAGE 109

Step 2: Identify and Agree the Goals

Once you have agreed a topic for coaching and worked out in general what you want to achieve, you need to agree the goals for the assignment and also, when working through the assignment, for each coaching session.

A good coaching assignment must always benefit the person concerned by developing their skills but it must also provide valuable outcomes in work areas.

Ask yourself, what are the benefits for:

- the person being coached?
- their team or department?
- other colleagues/suppliers?
- customers?
- the organization as a whole?

In setting your own goals for the assignment, you should also ask yourself the following questions:

- What is to be achieved?
- Why it is important?
- How is it to be achieved?
- How will achievement be measured?
- When are the goals to be achieved?
- Who is involved?

YOU MAY NOW CONTINUE WITH THE NEXT FAST TRACK SECTION ON PAGE 103
OR MOVE TO THE SKILLBUILDER EXERCISE ON PAGE 110

Step 3: Explore the Current Position

Remember: The coach listens and observes for 80 per cent of the time.

FAST TRACK

Coaching is all about developing a person's skills while getting work done at the same time. In each assignment you therefore need to explore:

- the person's current skill gap
- the work and tasks that have to be completed.

In exploring the current situation, whether it is at the beginning of an assignment or as a means of confirming progress in a coaching session, the most important skill is that of asking the right type of questions.

ASK THE RIGHT QUESTIONS

There are two main types of questions both of which have a role to play in coaching: open and closed

Open questions Use these to open up a discussion or to probe more deeply into a particular area. They usually start with 'How?', 'What?' and 'Who?'. A balanced mix of open and closed questions can help you pace the direction and flow of conversation to achieve specific ends.

Open questions are typically used to:

- gain additional **information** – '*What has pleased you most about . . . ?*'
- find out about the other person's **feelings** – '*What do you feel about this option . . .?*'
- probe more **deeply** – '*Why do you feel it won't work . . .?*'.

Closed questions Use these when you want to direct discussion into a particular area, confirm the accuracy of information, clarify assumptions or test the commitment of the other person. They typically start with words such as 'Can?' 'Are?' 'Do?' 'Is?' and 'Which?'.

Closed questions are typically used to:

- **clarify** or **confirm** the accuracy of information or a person's understanding – '*Is it right that . . .?*'
- gain **commitment** – '*Are we agreed then . . . ?*'

YOU MAY NOW CONTINUE WITH THE NEXT FAST TRACK SECTION ON PAGE 104
OR MOVE TO THE SKILLBUILDER EXERCISE ON PAGE 111

FAST TRACK

Step 4: Explore the Options

Having assessed the current situation, you must now jointly explore options and develop a range of ideas for progressing the session and, ultimately, the assignment.

When we react we focus on the person. When we respond we focus on the issue.

In addition to questioning, a key skill at this stage is to listen actively and respond appropriately so that the other person can:

- confirm their existing knowledge
- explore their understanding.

LISTEN ACTIVELY

You cannot be a good coach if you don't understand the other person's point of view. To do that you must listen to them and absorb what they say.

Listening is an act of generosity; it helps others to think through their ideas. As someone once said, 'How do I know what I think, until I hear what I say?'.

There are five rules for active listening:

- Be still – give the other person 'space' to talk.
- Show interest – encourage the other person to 'open up'.
- Ask questions **and** acknowledge the answers.
- Reflect back what the other person says in order to check your own understanding.
- Summarize to check that you both agree about the discussion.

RESPOND

Responding and reacting may sound like the same thing but they're not – and the difference between them can be crucial to your ability to coach successfully.

- **Reactions** are often our automatic reflexes.
- **Responses** are our considered and thought-out actions.

It takes a great deal of self-discipline to respond rather than react. It prevents:

- saying things in the heat of the moment that can have a damaging effect on outcomes and other people
- having to spend time undoing all the damage caused.

YOU MAY NOW CONTINUE WITH THE NEXT FAST TRACK SECTION ON PAGE 105
OR MOVE TO THE SKILLBUILDER EXERCISE ON PAGE 112

Step 5: Develop an Action Plan

You have confirmed the goals for the assignment, decided upon the goal for the session, explored the current situation and the options available. Next, you need to develop an action plan to carry you through to your next session.

The coaching process may take place over a period of months and is likely to contain several coaching sessions. This is why a clear action plan is necessary to help keep the coaching assignment on course and to act as a starting point for reviewing progress in each coaching session. In developing this action plan, make sure that you have answers to the questions you will find in the framework in the accompanying Skillbuilder.

The coach and the coached both need to agree and understand the demands of the action plan and you need to build on it during each coaching session.

Below is an example of an action plan developed by someone undertaking a coaching assignment which will enable them to take responsibility for the department's stock control system in three months' time. You could develop one of your own using these headings.

Coaching Session Dates	Action Steps	Degree of Authority Required	Support Available From	Measures of Success Will be	Completed and Reviewed by
Session 1	Understand the principles of the stock control system		Manager	Team presentation	15/7
Session 2	Generate stock summary reports on daily, weekly, monthly basis	Level 1 Access	Stock manager	Reports delivered on time	31/7
Session 3	Run daily monitoring system and list items for re-ordering	Level 2 Access	Manager	Error-free stock-out lists	4/9
Session 4	Reorder flagged low-level stock items	Level 3 Access	Manager	Stock-outs eliminated	1/10
Session 5	Run the stock monitoring system for a week unassisted	Level 4 Access	Manager	Smooth running of stock system	29/10

YOU MAY NOW CONTINUE WITH THE NEXT FAST TRACK SECTION ON PAGE 106
OR MOVE TO THE SKILLBUILDER EXERCISE ON PAGE 113

Step 6: Give Authority to Act

In coaching you have to take the plunge and let the other person get on with it. This includes **giving the freedom to make mistakes**. Structuring the assignment into a number of coaching sessions will enable you to limit the possibilities of huge errors.

You still have overall responsibility and must make judgements about how much authority to delegate and what resources they will need. However, if you have followed the previous five steps, you will be in a position to give the person genuine responsibility.

You will have to define the authority clearly. The person being coached may be required to take responsibility for:

- budgets and financial resources
- other people's time
- other people
- customer service issues
- systems.

Once this is done all you need do is: **let go but keep in touch**.

YOU MAY NOW CONTINUE WITH THE NEXT FAST TRACK SECTION ON PAGE 107
OR MOVE TO THE SKILLBUILDER EXERCISE ON PAGE 114

FAST TRACK

Step 7: Summarize the Session

At the end of each coaching session it is very important that the person being coached fully understands what is being asked of them, so always check their level of understanding. A key skill in doing this is to paraphrase and reflect back what the other person has said.

Reflecting back to people what they have said can be a great help in enabling them to understand an issue or problem for themselves. How often have you heard people say 'Just talking about it has helped'?

PARAPHRASE AND REFLECT

The role of the coach is to mirror the thoughts, feelings and ideas of the other person so that they can:

- gain perspective
- gain insight
- think their thoughts through.

Paraphrasing and reflecting back what you have heard allows you to confirm that you:

- have heard
- are listening
- have understood.

It will also provide:

- a useful marker for where you are in the discussion
- a useful summary of an idea or topic on your meeting agenda
- a means of moving on to the next topic
- a link between ideas.

In paraphrasing it's useful to begin with such phrases as:

- *'So what you are saying is . . .'*
- *'So what you feel is that . . .'*
- *'The most important issue for you seems to be . . .'*

YOU MAY NOW CONTINUE WITH THE NEXT FAST TRACK SECTION ON PAGE 123
OR MOVE TO THE SKILLBUILDER EXERCISE ON PAGE 116

Step 1: Identify and Jointly Agree the Topic

Next you should jointly agree the topic. Use Step 1 of the framework for identifying the important things to cover and to agree a topic for the coaching assignment.

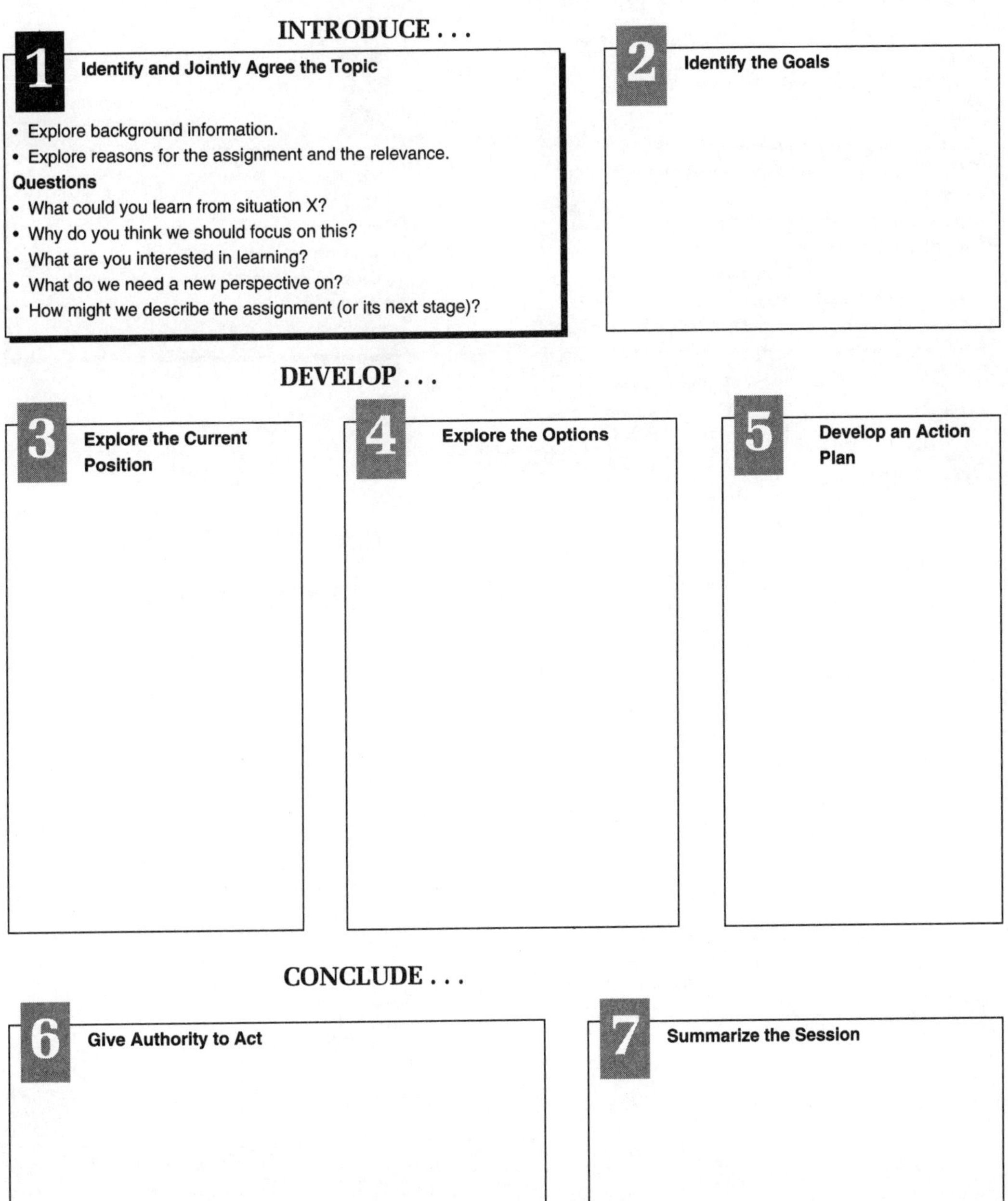

SKILLBUILDER

Step 2: Identify and Agree the Goals

For the coaching assignment and for each coaching session you will need to identify goals. Use the actions and questions below to keep you focused on this important stage of the coaching process.

INTRODUCE . . .

1 Identify and Jointly Agree the Topic

- Explore background information.
- Explore reasons for the assignment and the relevance.

Questions

- What could you learn from situation X?
- Why do you think we should focus on this?
- What are you interested in learning?
- What do we need a new perspective on?
- How might we describe the assignment (or its next stage)?

2 Identify the Goals

- Confirm long-term goals – for the assignment.
- Develop short-term goals – for the coaching session.

Questions

- What do you need to know, discuss, plan, consider in order to complete this assignment?
- What do we want to achieve from this particular session?

DEVELOP . . .

3 Explore the Current Position

4 Explore the Options

5 Develop an Action Plan

CONCLUDE . . .

6 Give Authority to Act

7 Summarize the Session

REMEMBER:
- **Ask questions.**
- **Show interest and listen.**
- **Paraphrase.**
- **Focus on the other person.**
- **Encourage.**

Step 3: Explore the Current Position

When exploring the current situation in a coaching session, you need to cover the following areas and ask the following questions.

INTRODUCE . . .

1 Identify and Jointly Agree the Topic

- Explore background information.
- Explore reasons for the assignment and the relevance.

Questions
- What could you learn from situation X?
- Why do you think we should focus on this?
- What are you interested in learning?
- What do we need a new perspective on?
- How might we describe the assignment (or its next stage)?

2 Identify the Goals

- Confirm long-term goals – for the assignment.
- Develop short-term goals – for the coaching session.

Questions
- What do you need to know, discuss, plan, consider in order to complete this assignment?
- What do we want to achieve from this particular session?

DEVELOP . . .

3 Explore the Current Position

- Ask for ideas.
- Encourage the other person to think for themselves.
- Establish existing knowledge/experience.
- Discuss objectives.

Questions
- What do you already know/do regarding this issue?
- What initial ideas can you think of for this stage of the assignment?
- What has happened in the past?
- Who else is involved in this?
- What do they think?
- What do you think will be most difficult?
- What do you think will be easier?

4 Explore the Options

5 Develop an Action Plan

CONCLUDE . . .

6 Give Authority to Act

7 Summarize the Session

SKILLBUILDER

REMEMBER:
- **Ask questions.**
- **Listen.**
- **Make suggestions.**

Step 4: Explore the Options

When exploring the options in a coaching session, you will need to consider the actions and ask questions in step 4.

INTRODUCE . . .

1 Identify and Jointly Agree the Topic

- Explore background information.
- Explore reasons for the assignment and the relevance.

Questions
- What could you learn from situation X?
- Why do you think we should focus on this?
- What are you interested in learning?
- What do we need a new perspective on?
- How might we describe the assignment (or its next stage)?

2 Identify the Goals

- Confirm long-term goals – for the assignment.
- Develop short-term goals – for the coaching session.

Questions
- What do you need to know, discuss, plan, consider in order to complete this assignment?
- What do we want to achieve from this particular session?

SKILLBUILDER

DEVELOP . . .

3 Explore the Current Position

- Ask for ideas.
- Encourage the other person to think for themselves.
- Establish existing knowledge/experience.
- Discuss objectives.

Questions
- What do you already know/do regarding this issue?
- What initial ideas can you think of for this stage of the assignment?
- What has happened in the past?
- Who else is involved in this?
- What do they think?
- What do you think will be most difficult?
- What do you think will be easier?

4 Explore the Options

- Help the other person to think through their ideas.
- Share your experiences.
- Show by example.
- Discuss constraints, demands and implications of the assignment.
- Discuss alternative methods and approaches.

Questions
- What options could we consider here?
- Can we prioritize them?
- Which do you think is the best option and why?
- What will you need to help you?
- Can we improve on this?
- I have some experience of this – would it be helpful to tell you about it?

5 Develop an Action Plan

CONCLUDE . . .

6 Give Authority to Act

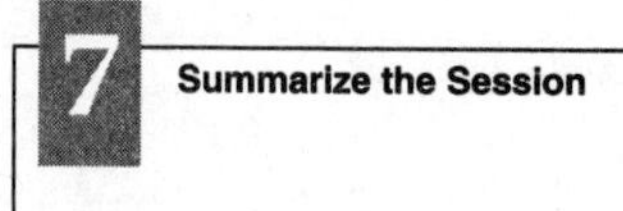

7 Summarize the Session

REMEMBER:
- **Ask questions.**
- **Make suggestions.**

Step 5: Develop an Action Plan

When developing an action plan during a coaching session, you will need to formulate the specific actions that will take you forward to your next session. Following the actions and questions in the framework will help you keep on track.

INTRODUCE . . .

1 Identify and Jointly Agree the Topic

- Explore background information.
- Explore reasons for the assignment and the relevance.

Questions
- What could you learn from situation X?
- Why do you think we should focus on this?
- What are you interested in learning?
- What do we need a new perspective on?
- How might we describe the assignment (or its next stage)?

2 Identify the Goals

- Confirm long-term goals – for the assignment.
- Develop short-term goals – for the coaching session.

Questions
- What do you need to know, discuss, plan, consider in order to complete this assignment?
- What do we want to achieve from this particular session?

DEVELOP . . .

3 Explore the Current Position

- Ask for ideas.
- Encourage the other person to think for themselves.
- Establish existing knowledge/experience.
- Discuss objectives.

Questions
- What do you already know/do regarding this issue?
- What initial ideas can you think of for this stage of the assignment?
- What has happened in the past?
- Who else is involved in this?
- What do they think?
- What do you think will be most difficult?
- What do you think will be easier?

4 Explore the Options

- Help the other person to think through their ideas.
- Share your experiences.
- Show by example.
- Discuss constraints, demands and implications of the assignment.
- Discuss alternative methods and approaches.

Questions
- What options could we consider here?
- Can we prioritize them?
- Which do you think is the best option and why?
- What will you need to help you?
- Can we improve on this?
- I have some experience of this – would it be helpful to tell you about it?

5 Develop an Action Plan

- Establish what is to be done.
- Decide when it is to be done by.
- Establish the authority required.

Questions
- What needs to be done?
- When can you achieve this by?
- How will we monitor or check progress?
- What problems do you foresee?
- What authority will you need for this stage?
- Have you the right resources and support?
- How will it fit in with your other tasks?

CONCLUDE . . .

6 Give Authority to Act

7 Summarize the Session

Step 6: Give Authority to Act

First of all, define the authority the person being coached will need and consider what resources they will require.

AUTHORITY CHECK	
Delegated status and responsibility will be required for . . .	
Financial resources required	
Time budget needed	
Allocation of the people and roles required	
Space required	
Systems requirement	

Each coaching session you have during the assignment will need to define the exact authority required for the person to carry out the next stage of the assignment. You should take two important actions here.

1. Make sure that the individual has the authority to perform, and that colleagues and managers are informed and therefore recognize their authority.
2. Limit that authority to the task in hand. It's the key way for you to control the assignment. Give authority for the next relevant stage only.

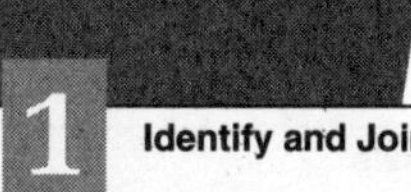

REMEMBER:

- **Listen and observe for 80 per cent of the time.**
- **Don't impose your own ideas.**

INTRODUCE . . .

1 Identify and Jointly Agree the Topic

- Explore background information.
- Explore reasons for the assignment and the relevance.

Questions

- What could you learn from situation X?
- Why do you think we should focus on this?
- What are you interested in learning?
- What do we need a new perspective on?
- How might we describe the assignment (or its next stage)?

2 Identify the Goals

- Confirm long-term goals – for the assignment.
- Develop short-term goals – for the coaching session.

Questions

- What do you need to know, discuss, plan, consider in order to complete this assignment?
- What do we want to achieve from this particular session?

DEVELOP . . .

3 Explore the Current Position

- Ask for ideas.
- Encourage the other person to think for themselves.
- Establish existing knowledge/experience.
- Discuss objectives.

Questions

- What do you already know/do regarding this issue?
- What initial ideas can you think of for this stage of the assignment?
- What has happened in the past?
- Who else is involved in this?
- What do they think?
- What do you think will be most difficult?
- What do you think will be easier?

4 Explore the Options

- Help the other person to think through their ideas.
- Share your experiences.
- Show by example.
- Discuss constraints, demands and implications of the assignment.
- Discuss alternative methods and approaches.

Questions

- What options could we consider here?
- Can we prioritize them?
- Which do you think is the best option and why?
- What will you need to help you?
- Can we improve on this?
- I have some experience of this – would it be helpful to tell you about it?

5 Develop an Action Plan

- Establish what is to be done.
- Decide when it is to be done by.
- Establish the authority required.

Questions

- What needs to be done?
- When can you achieve this by?
- How will we monitor or check progress?
- What problems do you foresee?
- What authority will you need for this stage?
- Have you the right resources and support?
- How will it fit in with your other tasks?

CONCLUDE . . .

6 Give Authority to Act

- Fix it and clear it now so the other person can act on your behalf.

Questions

- What support will you need?
- What authority do you think you need to complete this stage?
- What do I (the coach) need to fix in order for you to do this?

7 Summarize the Session

Step 7: Summarize the Session

Finally, each coaching session should be clearly summarized. This allows us to look back and understand what has taken place. Use the questions below to help you. Use this completed framework as a checklist in your coaching sessions.

INTRODUCE . . .

1 Identify and Jointly Agree the Topic

- Explore background information.
- Explore reasons for the assignment and the relevance.

Questions

- What could you learn from situation X?
- Why do you think we should focus on this?
- What are you interested in learning?
- What do we need a new perspective on?
- How might we describe the assignment (or its next stage)?

2 Identify the Goals

- Confirm long-term goals – for the assignment.
- Develop short-term goals – for the coaching session.

Questions

- What do you need to know, discuss, plan, consider in order to complete this assignment?
- What do we want to achieve from this particular session?

DEVELOP . . .

3 Explore the Current Position

- Ask for ideas.
- Encourage the other person to think for themselves.
- Establish existing knowledge/experience.
- Discuss objectives.

Questions

- What do you already know/do regarding this issue?
- What initial ideas can you think of for this stage of the assignment?
- What has happened in the past?
- Who else is involved in this?
- What do they think?
- What do you think will be most difficult?
- What do you think will be easier?

4 Explore the Options

- Help the other person to think through their ideas.
- Share your experiences.
- Show by example.
- Discuss constraints, demands and implications of the assignment.
- Discuss alternative methods and approaches.

Questions

- What options could we consider here?
- Can we prioritize them?
- Which do you think is the best option and why?
- What will you need to help you?
- Can we improve on this?
- I have some experience of this – would it be helpful to tell you about it?

5 Develop an Action Plan

- Establish what is to be done.
- Decide when it is to be done by.
- Establish the authority required.

Questions

- What needs to be done?
- When can you achieve this by?
- How will we monitor or check progress?
- What problems do you foresee?
- What authority will you need for this stage?
- Have you the right resources and support?
- How will it fit in with your other tasks?

CONCLUDE . . .

6 Give Authority to Act

- Fix it and clear it now so the other person can act on your behalf.

Questions

- What support will you need?
- What authority do you think you need to complete this stage?
- What do I (the coach) need to fix in order for you to do this?

7 Summarize the Session

- Summarize the agreed action points.
- Set the time and agenda for the next meeting.

Questions

- What have we agreed at this meeting?
- What are the next steps in this project?
- When shall we have the next coaching session?

ACTION POINTS

Use this blank framework to plan and record each coaching session. You can note down important points and questions.

A FRAMEWORK FOR COACHING OTHERS

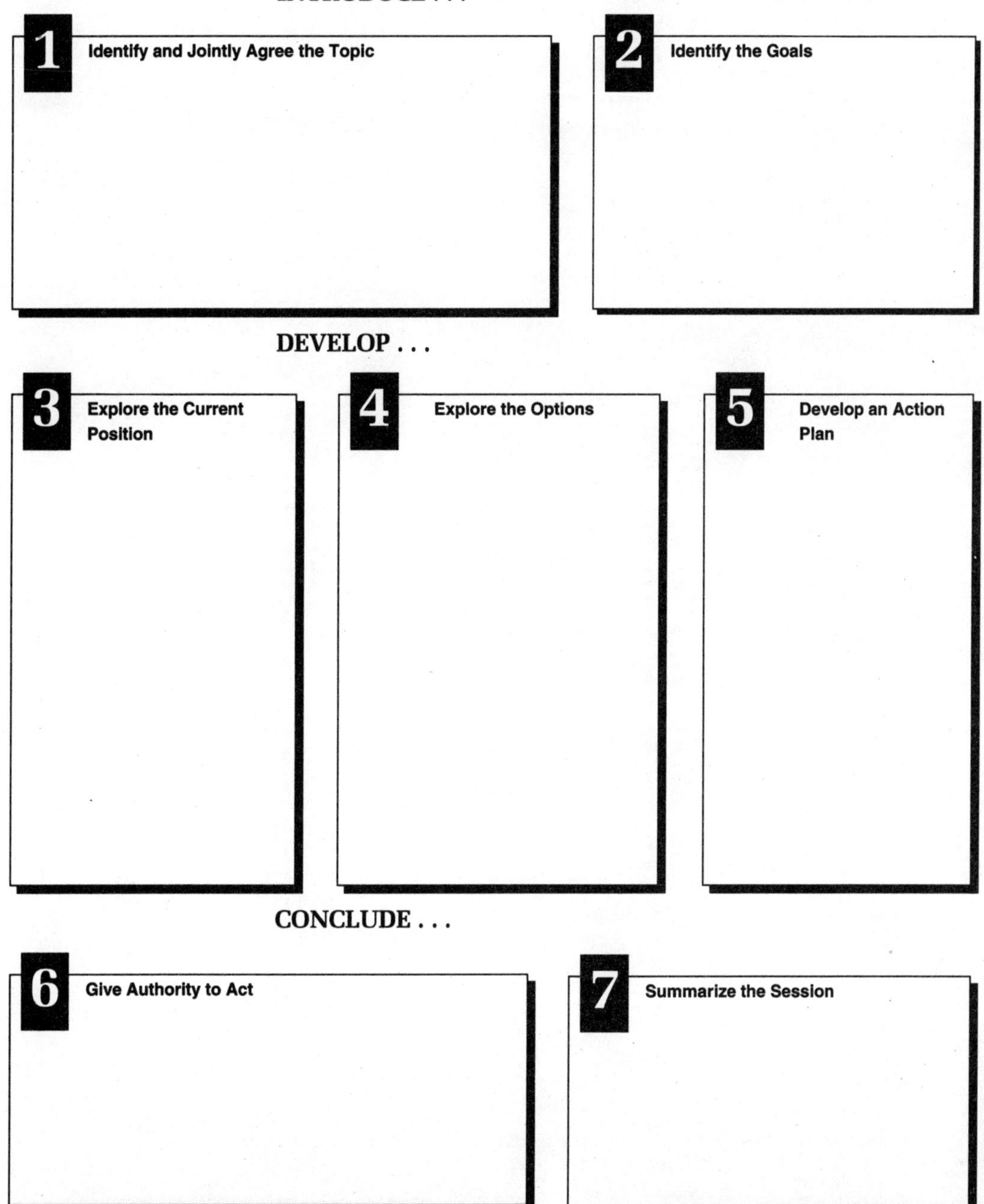

PART IV Recognizing Success

Thanking and recognizing people for good performance is the theme of the final Part of this Workbook. Goal-setting, coaching and feedback will enable you to gift-wrap the job for your team members. Part IV, 'Recognizing Success', will show you how to tag it with praise.

Giving thanks and recognizing good performance is critical to ensuring that the goals of the organization, the department and the individual are:

- recognized and
- rewarded.

Part IV will help you to manage the performance of people at work by giving you:

- quick access to the skills involved in informally rewarding people for good performance.
- insights and practical ideas for recognizing good performance at work in all sorts of ways.

UNIT 8 Recognizing Individual Performance

In this unit you will consider:

- **how you currently thank individuals for good performance**
- **a variety of opportunities and methods for saying 'thank you'**
- **powerful ways to say 'thank you'.**

There are many ways of recognizing good performance and what may be appropriate at any time will depend on:

- the personalities involved
- the significance of the performance.

However, you must remember that all good performance is important and should therefore be recognized. A little praise, frequently given, is probably more effective than a lot and seldom. It is difficult for someone to feel motivated on the strength of one 'thank you' at the annual performance review. Waiting a year for the next 'thank you' is demoralizing.

Thanking People for Good Performance

You should vary the ways in which you give thanks for good performance to suit individuals and circumstances. A sense of surprise is an important part of motivation. Small informal gestures of thanks are always appreciated, so gift-wrap the job and tag it with praise.

Managers have the following opportunities for giving thanks.

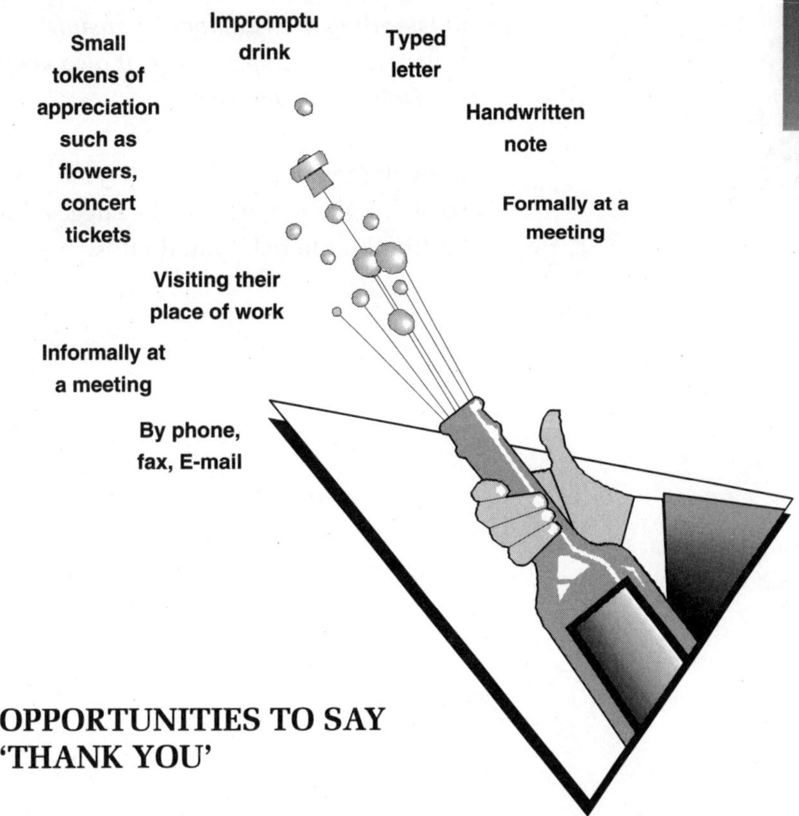

OPPORTUNITIES TO SAY 'THANK YOU'

Receiving spontaneous thanks is one of the most powerful motivators; people often highly value being recognized or rewarded for their outstanding performance at the time it occurs. Tom Peters recounts an example of one US company which built its recognition programme around a lapel pin featuring a banana because the CEO once spontaneously rewarded an employee for outstanding performance with the only item he could find in his desk at the time. (Peters, T. and Waterman, R., *In Search of Excellence*, Harper and Row, 1982.)

Even though your organization may have a formal reward system you should consider how to recognize outstanding performance on a spontaneous basis. It is more immediate, more personal and more motivational. Sending a handwritten letter to the individual, creating peer recognition through the team's bulletin board, or sending a present to the individual's social partner are all effective ways of spontaneously providing thanks for past performance and motivating future effort.

One UK CEO holds celebration breakfasts once or twice a month to thank those individuals who have produced outstanding performance or sustained effort. Not only is this a way of recognizing success, it also keeps the CEO in touch with the feelings of key staff.

But before you can say 'thank you', you have to have something to praise. Use the suggestions in the next Skillbuilder to help you do this.

YOU MAY NOW CONTINUE WITH THE NEXT FAST TRACK SECTION ON PAGE 125
OR MOVE TO THE SKILLBUILDER EXERCISE ON PAGE 127

Celebrating Individual Success

The verbal or written 'thank you' is important but there will be occasions when you want to celebrate success and create special memories.

There are many ideas you can try:

- **Family rewards**. Families are often the unrecognized supporters of good performance. Thanking them can be even more motivational than rewarding the employee alone. You could send them a gift or provide for a family day out. But consider the type of reward carefully. Tickets to an important football match would delight a family of football fans; a day at the races might not.
- **Formal events**. A dinner, celebration lunch or champagne breakfast help to give your thanks a special glow.
- **Job swaps/shadowing**. An individual could become a director or manager for a day, or accompany one.
- **Financial reward**. A small or large financial reward given spontaneously, rather than through a planned or structured scheme, sends motivation soaring.
- **Making a dream come true**. Many people have something they dream of doing or owning. Arrange for the hire of that special car for a week, that trip in a hot air balloon, that round of golf with a celebrity . . . .

Make sure that each member of your team knows: We can't spell s ccess without U

YOU MAY NOW CONTINUE WITH THE NEXT FAST TRACK SECTION ON PAGE 133
OR MOVE TO THE SKILLBUILDER EXERCISE ON PAGE 128

Celebrating Individual Success

Ways to Say 'Thank You'

An individual's success becomes special and recognized when you put it in writing. Most people value a handwritten note or letter, but there are also other ways to say thank you. The Fast Track on page 125 identifies some of them.

Develop ideas of your own in the space below. Think also of the different opportunities you get to say thank you.

Opportunities to say thank you	**Ways to say thank you**
e.g. when the team is working late to meet a deadline.	Get a pizza delivered as a surprise – even better, deliver it yourself!
•	•
•	•
•	•
•	•

Remember. . .

- Recognize small successes as well as big ones.
- Thank people frequently – every little recognition is a positive stroke that makes a person feel recognized and rewarded.
- Make sure that people bump into good news all over the place – display good news in unexpected places.

Thank you

From the ____________

For ____________

Name ____________

❑ Sales
❑ Restaurant
❑ House Keeping
❑ Reception
❑ General Manager
❑ Maintenance
❑ Head Office
❑ Kitchen

Success Notes

Design preprinted compliment notes for recognizing success. Have a pad of 'You've made my day' Post-its to say a personal 'Thank you'.

SKILLBUILDER

Celebrating Individual Success

Consider each of the 'thank you' events below. If you feel that any are relevant, make notes on how you could organize them.

Space has been left for you to add more ideas.

I could	**I could organize it by . . .**
• give family rewards	
• arrange a formal event	
• organize a job swap	
• give a spontaneous financial reward	
• make someone's dream come true	
•	
•	
•	
•	
•	

SKILLBUILDER

Recognizing Individual Performance

- *'Men will go to war for a flag and give up their lives for a piece of ribbon'* – don't forget the power of recognizing success with symbols of thanks.
- Memories are made from celebrations and tokens of thanks. It's public affirmation of your worth. After all, don't you have a box tucked away at home with form badges, certificates and memorabilia of your success from your schooldays onwards?
- The frequency of thanks is important: little and often reassures and satisfies.
- Thoughtful thanks flatter. Think carefully what kind of recognition would be appreciated by the individual concerned. Personalize the reward. Giving everyone a gift token at Christmas is a ritual not a personal 'thank you'.

ACTION POINTS

If I was to give each person in my team an appropriate gift the list would be:

-
-
-
-

UNIT 9 Recognizing Team Performance

In this unit we will consider:

- **different ways in which you can thank your team and encourage them to thank each other**
- **ways to track the successes of your team**
- **events that will celebrate your team's success**

Because it takes time and trouble to build an effective team it's important to keep the team healthy and its collective self-esteem high by giving it quality attention and recognizing its successes.

Recognize your team's success in an appropriate manner. Give different thanks to different team. Consider how you might reward the following three teams, each appreciating a different kind of recognition.

- **A team that works like a boat crew.**
  A group of people with a clear objective (destination) each having a defined but limited job and under the direct control of a captain. This team would appreciate the following kind of recognition . . .

- **A team that works like an orchestra.**
  A group of different professionals. Their leader co-ordinates their performance in order to harmonize their individual efforts. This team would appreciate the following kind of recognition . . .

- **A team that works like a group of missionaries.**
  A group of people who go into the 'field' to do their work and may have very little interaction with each other. They communicate through a leader. What binds them is a shared set of values or skills. This team would appreciate the following kind of recognition . . .

Ways to Say 'Thank You'

Sometimes it is the way people are or the way they do their work that you might want to recognize rather than the completion of a particular task. People are different and bring a certain set of valuable attributes to the work of the team but you may have to tease out what these are.

ALL TOGETHER BETTER
Our success together is a reflection of our individuality.

You should find ways of discovering what you and each member of your team particularly value about each other. One way to do this is to bring the team together and encourage them to thank each other for their individual contributions. Use the next Skillbuilder to structure this activity.

YOU MAY NOW CONTINUE WITH THE NEXT FAST TRACK SECTION ON PAGE 134
OR MOVE TO THE SKILLBUILDER EXERCISE ON PAGE 137

Ways to Track Success

You may want to create a more systematic way of recording and tracking successes by setting up a team success system. The following Skillbuilder shows you how to set up a balance sheet system.

The benefits of such a system are that it:

- focuses individuals on team success
- recognizes the contribution of the full team
- encourages teams to deliver extra performance
- provides a mechanism for measuring that contribution
- creates positive competition between teams.

Teams could also track their own success with a 'Boasting' board on which they post their view of success. This will give you useful feedback on how they define success.

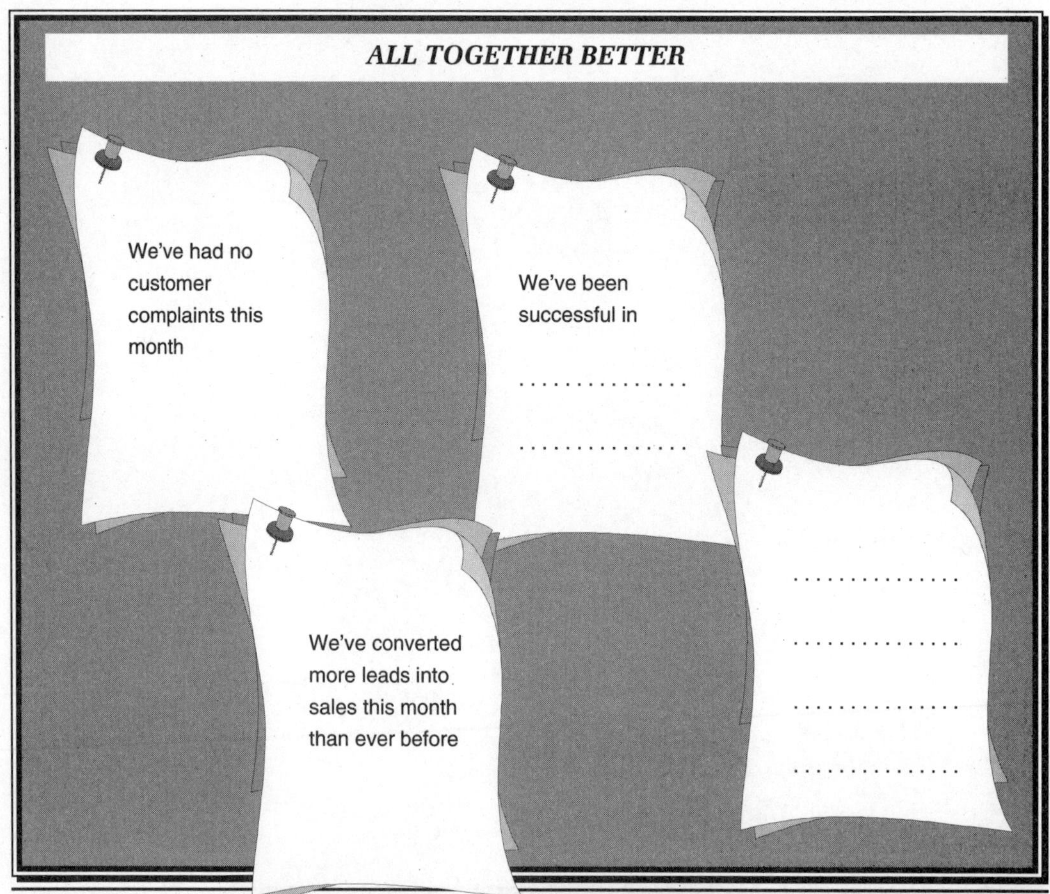

YOU MAY NOW CONTINUE WITH THE NEXT FAST TRACK SECTION ON PAGE 135 OR MOVE TO THE SKILLBUILDER EXERCISE ON PAGE 138

Celebrate Team Success

There will be occasions when you want to celebrate team success, creating special memories and enhancing the team's commitment.

There are many ideas you can try with your team.

REGULAR REVIVAL HOUR
Gather the team together when they've been under pressure to thank them and to use the opportunity to discuss customer complaints, new business, new ideas and deadlines managed effectively.

- **Team rewards**. Teams which have performed particularly well could receive recognition and thanks by means of an outing. Give the trip focus by linking it to a business opportunity, training and development opportunities or competitor visits. Alternatively, even take the team and their families on an outing.
- **A regular Team Success Column**. Such a column in the newsletter would give teams a success profile and would enable you to build up a scrapbook of successful stories.
- **Formal events**. A dinner, celebration lunch or champagne breakfast help give your thanks some sparkle.
- **Visits**. The team could receive, or make a special visit to, a director. This should not be just a head round the door 'Thanks, guys' but one where the director spends time working with the team.
- **Community projects**. Sponsor a local event or charity of your team's choosing and allow the team to work on the project.

YOU MAY NOW CONTINUE WITH THE MAINTAINING YOUR SKILL SECTION ON PAGE 143
OR MOVE TO THE SKILLBUILDER EXERCISE ON PAGE 139

Ways to Say 'Thank You'

1. Bring the team together.
2. Explain that this is an informal activity in which we can communicate clearly to each other the positive attributes each member brings to their work.
3. Ask each person to write their name on top of a copy of the activity chart (see below) and pass it on to the person next to them. Each person in the group must then contribute to each individual's chart as follows.
4. Ask each person to fill in the activity sheet from the bottom and then fold under the portion they have completed and pass it on to the next person and so on.
5. When everyone has contributed to each person's activity sheet ask for the sheets to be passed back to the person it belongs to. They can then unfold the sheet, read it and compare comments.
6. Add value to this process for your team and summarize. Then describe the team's purpose, role and achievements.

Name:

Your role is important to our team because it enables us to . . . From . . .	The skills I most appreciate are . . . From . . .	Your personal qualities are . . . From . . .
Your role is important to our team because it enables us to . . . From . . .	The skills I most appreciate are . . . From . . .	Your personal qualities are . . . From . . .
Your role is important to our team because it enables us to . . . From . . .	The skills I most appreciate are . . . From . . .	Your personal qualities are . . . From . . .

Ways to Track Success

Use the **balance sheet** below to credit and debit team success.

1. Decide on the jobs tasks and areas of responsibility you want to focus success on. Examples could be items delivered on time, number of customer complaints/compliments.
2. Decide on a scoring system that measures success. Example credits and debits could be as follows:
   - Customer thanks +100
   - Customer complaint -100
   - Customer criticism -50
   - Customer requests for a particular person +50
   - Weekly targets met +50 each
3. Decide what the points will earn in teams of reward. For example 500 points might win a certain number of store vouchers or a team meal.
4. Decide the timeframe over which you will make the awards.
5. Design a score sheet like the example below.
6. Decide how you will feed results back to team(s).
7. Brief your team(s) well in advance of starting the system, explaining the benefits, how the system works, the timeframe and so on.
8. Appoint a coordinator to collate data.

SKILLBUILDER

BALANCE SHEET FOR SUCCESS

Job Task/Responsibility	Week/Month 1		Week/Month 2		Week/Month 3		Week/Month 4	
	Credit	Debit	Credit	Debit	Credit	Debit	Credit	Debit
1.								
2.								
3.								
4.								
5.								
6.								
7.								
8.								
9.								
TOTAL								

Celebrate Team Success

Consider each of the 'thank you' events below. If you feel any are relevant, make notes on how you could implement these for the team. Space has been left for you to add more ideas.

I could	I could organize it by . . .
• give team rewards	
• develop a team success column in our newsletter	
• arrange VIP visits	
• arrange a formal team event	
• give a spontaneous financial reward to the team	
• encourage the team to support a community project	
• • • •	

SKILLBUILDER

Recognizing Team Success

- Celebrating the team's success will help members feel positive towards their team and to own their success.
- Teams are collections of differences so you should also let each individual know how they have contributed to the success of that team and why they are valued as a team member.

ACTION POINTS

If I was to consider one way of recognizing and celebrating my team's success it would be to:

Maintaining Your Skill

In order to maintain the skills you have built while completing this book you might like to consider using the ideas described below.

MANAGE YOUR OWN MENTORING

Find someone you can talk to. You could identify someone by using this checklist.

Type of Support	At my Job	Away from my Job
• Someone I can learn from		
• Someone with whom I can discuss the self-help exercises I have completed		
• Someone who helps me focus on my strengths		
• Someone who gives me constructive feedback		
• Someone who is always a source of valuable information		
• Someone who will challenge me to take a good look at myself		
• Someone I can share my disappointments with		
• Someone I can share my successes with		
• Someone who introduces me to new ideas, new interests, new people		
• Someone I can confide in		

POST-IT FOR SUCCESS

The last thing you do is the first thing you remember. Create a poster with a summary of all the Action Points you have identified. Keep it in front of you. Change its position weekly and rewrite it monthly. Familiarity breeds forgetfulness.

Extending Your Knowledge

You may like to extend your knowledge further by exploring some of the sources indicated in this mind map. You could develop this mind map further using your own sources.

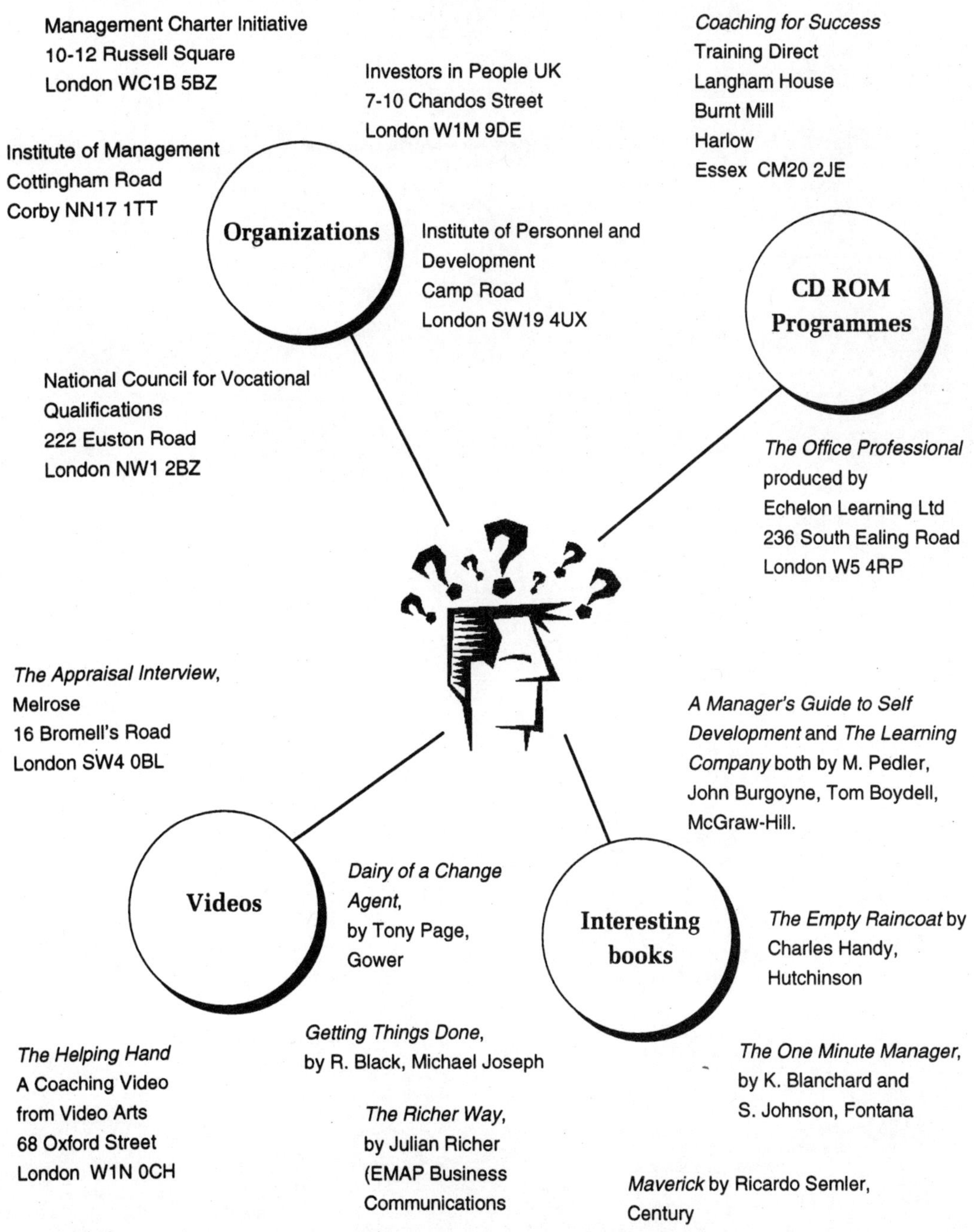